Richard Landerman

Illustrated by Denise Crane

The Fly Rod Chronicles

A Collection of Essays on the Quiet Sport of Fly Fishing

Sortis Publishing

© 2007 Richard Landerman

All rights reserved. No part of this book may be reproduced or transmitted in any form or by any means, electronic or mechanical, including photocopying, recording, or by any information storage and retrieval system, without permission in writing from the publisher, Sortis Publishing. Visit us at www.sortispublishing.com

ISBN 13# 9780977202522

Printed in the United States of America.

Dedicated to Janet, my luckiest catch ever, and to our spawn: Amy, Heather, Mark, Kristen, Erin and Drew.

Contents

ii	Acknowledgements
iv	Foreword
v	Introduction
1	What's the Point?
7	First Fly Rod
17	It Always Rains On My Day Off
25	January 6
33	Band Of Brothers
47	What's the Point?
55	You Never Have Any Fun
67	Lemon Meringue Pie
77	The Moustache Factor
91	A Pretty Dry State
103	Combat Pay
115	Old Spice
127	Restoring The Rapidan
139	Fly Fishing Las Vegas
145	Teach A Man To Fish...
151	Just An Average Fly Fisherman
163	Band Of Brothers
175	Menu Fishing
187	International Diplomacy —A Modest Proposal
193	Of Dentists' Chairs, Saddles, Waders...Things
195	Matthew
201	When I Go

Acknowledgements

No work like this is possible without a lot of help and I'm grateful to the many people who contributed to make this book possible. I hesitate to single out individuals for fear I may leave someone out; so if I forget to thank anyone who had anything to do with this book or its ideas, please know it wasn't done intentionally and I apologize for the oversight.

I'd like to thank, first of all, my wife, Janet; without her help as my editor (one of the best "red pencils" I know) and her encouragement, this book would not have happened. To all the English and writing teachers who influenced me from a young age—Pat Morgan, LaVon Rodsater, Harold Hill, Marilyn Arnold and many others, wherever you are—thanks.

Thanks to my friend, mentor, and great writer, Bill Ransom. To all the great fly fishermen and women and outdoor writers I have admired over the years—you have been an inspiration. Special thanks to Denise Crane for her beautiful illustrations; and much appreciation to Brian Hazelgren, who introduced me to Mike Webb, my publisher; and to Cecily Markland, whose final edit provided valuable contributions.

Thanks to my departed Dad, who helped me catch my first fish. Thanks, too, to my brothers and assorted others who I fished with through the years or who helped me learn fly fishing (some I mention in this book, some names I can't easily remember).

Thanks also to the many fly-fishing guides and boat

Acknowledgements

captains; to Ron Sharp for supplying me with a dazzling collection of soft-hackle flies and nymphs; and to my friend, Leo deMonbreun, who taught me the difference between ordinary and truly great bamboo fly rods. And, thanks to all the fish—bluegills, catfish, trout, steelhead, bass, halibut, barracuda, red snapper, stripers, salmon—that let me practice on them.

Foreword

Fly fishing is an appropriate metaphor for Richard Landerman's graceful, supple prose. He wields a captivating and rhythmic line of words and images that drifts us through both inner and outer riffles of complex human relationships. His fishing detail is scrupulously accurate, but *Fly Rod Chronicles* is no mere fishing tale. Pack up a good six-weight and wade on in!

— BILL RANSOM
Academic Dean of Curriculum and Professor of English
Evergreen State College
Olympia, Washington

Introduction

A library full of books and articles has been written on the subject of fly fishing, covering virtually every angle you can imagine. I even read one book from the point-of-view of the fish: sort of a fishy "Jonathan Livingston Seagull"—it was lame. So, why another fly-fishing book? Why *The Fly Rod Chronicles?*

The word "chronicle" connotes the telling of a tale, or a history, of a person or a people and their way of life. I wanted to tell my tale—a chronicle of how I grew up, the times and places; the people I knew—so my children or grandchildren would know what it was like when I was growing up.

I also wanted to chronicle, in a sketchy fashion, a modern history of the sport of fly fishing, at least the parts I have seen firsthand. When I was a kid, fly fishing was mostly for eccentrics or characters in stories. When you mentioned *fishing*, it was usually taken to mean with gear and bait. Yet, now (much like tennis, skiing and golf were in the preceding three decades), fly fishing, by large numbers of fly fisherpersons, has become the sport *du jour* of the '90s and the new millennium.

With the advance of science and technology, there's been a commensurate and not-so-subtle change in the technology, variety and quality of fishing equipment; and, the way all that new stuff is marketed to the fly-fishing public has become much more sophisticated, too.

Ditto the destinations and kinds of fly fishing: Alaska

Introduction

(salmon); Patagonia and New Zealand (trout); the Amazon (peacock bass); Scotland (steelhead and Atlantic salmon); Nova Scotia (Atlantic salmon and "bruiser" brook trout) and so on. Then there's the saltwater crowd: striper fishing off Martha's Vineyard; redfish off Corpus Christi; bonefish in the Bahamas. The list goes on and on. These are places that were maybe *heard* about decades ago when I was a kid, but they weren't necessarily associated with fly fishing until recent years.

I'm not what you'd call a neutral or disinterested chronicler. Far from it. I come at the job with attitudes, personal tastes, likes, dislikes, and observations that do come out in the book. That was intentional: On general principles, I can't stand government waste and senseless policies. I also hope I make clear my disagreement with a lot of the bad policy decisions of the current (and recent past) government administration, especially where ecology and wildlife management are concerned. I think similar attitudes, opinions, or points of view, held by others with whom I fish, also are reflected within these pages.

I don't make any claim that this is supposed to be a piece of objective, reporting-type journalism. (I do admit to occasional flutters of imagination; I am a fly fisherman, and we can't help fluffing things up a bit.).My only regret is that I didn't include more observations and opinions by others much smarter, wiser, and ecologically active than myself (and I know many).

I did consciously set out to show that fly fishing is *not* (and

Introduction

does not need to be) a mysterious, exotic, expensive sport, practiced only by effete snobs, intellectuals or weird wackos (although I've seen and met an abundance of real "characters" on and near the stream). I did want to show (1) that fly fishing *is* democratic: an equal opportunity sport, accessible to the average guy or gal of any age, race, or religion; (2) that it isn't hard to learn if you keep at it, and there are a lot of teachers, both public and private who are available and willing to help; (3) that, although you could spend a fortune on equipment and clothes if you want to, fly fishing does *not* necessarily need to be expensive to enjoy it to the fullest; (4) that there are plenty of fly-fishing venues within a reasonable casting distance (or, borrowing a different sporting metaphor, maybe within a one wood and nine iron shot) from your front porch, so you realty don't need to spend a lot of bucks on travel to enjoy some time spent on the water casting a fly, etc.

At any rate, that's some of my thinking as I finish this book. I reserve the right to change my mind about a few things and write a second book later on, if that monster Bow River brown doesn't drag me under first.

In the meantime, all the best—now, get out there and wet a line!

CHAPTER 1

What's the Point?

Part I

A couple of months ago my wife and I were at a social event. The wife of a friend, noticing my deeply tanned face, asked what I had been doing. My wife, Janet, jumped in before I could answer, and said, "He's just been *fly fishing* with his son for two days on the Green River." (As if fly fishing is a socially unacceptable pursuit.)

Then (to be friendly, I suppose) my friend's wife asked me what fly fishing was all about. I tried to explain the experience

The Fly Rod Chronicles

in a few words. I described the large, beautiful Green River rainbows, with their unique coloration and perfect black-pepper spotting. I described how clear the water is, so clear that the Green is called the "Aquarium." I mentioned how incredibly many fish we had seen and how that was probably an indication of the abundance of food.

She listened patiently, and asked, "Do you eat the fish you catch?"

I replied that I usually release the trout I catch.

She seemed surprised. "You mean you just let them *go*?"

I said, yes, I did.

"Then what's the point?" she asked.

Having never been asked this question about the sport I love, I was totally unprepared with a response. I just shrugged, grinned stupidly, felt the blush slowly burning under my new tan.

Janet poked me in the ribs. I'm glad *someone* enjoyed my embarrassment.

Since then, I've thought a lot about that question: "What's the point?"

I suppose, to the uninitiated, non-fly-fisher folk, it's a fair question. It ranks as a close relative to the query: Time Spent Fishing—Beneficial to Society or a Major Waste of Time? Not technical stuff, but a possible stumper, nonetheless.

I could have just blown off the woman's question with a withering, "You obviously don't fly fish do you?" But, that would only further the negative image we fly-fisher folk have as that of a gang of snobs.

What's the Point? – Part I

I also admit that I'm not very fast on my feet, never have been; and, as I get older, I get slower. Also, the woman and her husband *are* friends of ours, and I'm not really the mean-spirited type.

Still, I vowed, *Next time this happens (and there probably will be a next time), I'll be prepared with an arsenal of well-reasoned responses, complete with facts, anecdotes and witticisms to drive home my points.*

For example, for openers, I could respond with something like:

"What's the meaning of life?"

Or, "What's the point of smoking?"

Or. "What's the point of beauty pageants?"

Or, "What's the point of christening a ship?"

Or, "What's the point of naming dogs (or cats, or horses, or cars)?"

Next time, I'll try to point out that more than 65 million Americans bought fishing licenses last year. Do they know something that anyone who questions, "What's the point," doesn't?

Next time, I'll say that there are dozens of organizations, national and international (in Japan alone, I'm told, there are more than ten thousand such clubs), dedicated to the sport of fly fishing. With thousands of members. Surely, they must know something the questioners don't.

Next time, I'll say that many of these organizations donate hundreds of thousands of dollars and countless man hours to preserving and restoring fishing habitats, cleaning up around streams and parking areas, and mending fences for the landowners gracious enough to grant access to their private waters. Do they know something the uninformed don't?

I've seen the collective power, passion, and dedication of fly-fisher folk. Collectively, they've been able to change minds of politicians and courts to halt or change plans for mining, dams, and other projects that had serious potential to permanently damage our environment.

For example, in Montana, in the Jefferson River drainage area, the fly fishermen, landowners, and local politicians have managed to get together to work out their diverse demands and needs for the precious water. How was that possible? Was there something of value there that perhaps had a point to it?

Currently, as I'm in the process of writing this book, there's a concerted effort to halt a huge mining project planned for Alaska's Bristol Bay region. I hope the effort to stop it succeeds; it certainly has my support.

So, next time I'm asked, "What's the point," I'll say that many groups provide free classes and clinics at nominal cost or free of charge for beginners, especially women and children, who want to learn how to fly fish, Do they see the point?

Next time, I'll say that, locally, I've seen members of several such groups spend their weekends (when they themselves could have been out fishing) volunteering to assist fish and game people with fish-counting surveys or helping out at a community park on free fishing days for inner-city kids. What's the point to doing this?

Next time, I'll tell about how I fish the middle section of

What's the Point? – Part I

the Provo River more frequently than any other place. I hardly ever see any trash, empty cans, beer bottles, cigarette butts, bait boxes, or leader packages left carelessly scattered around; and when I do see anything like that, I pick it up and carry it out. I've seen other fly fishermen do the same thing. Why do we bother?

Next time I'm asked about the point of catching a fish, only to release it, I think I'll just casually throw in the most important reason to me: that if I kill it, I can never catch it again. If I release it back into the water, let it go, I may be able to catch that trout another time, when it's grown even bigger.

But, what's the point in doing that?

The Fly Rod Chronicles

Chapter 2

First Fly Rod

There's something special about that first fly rod. It's like Christmas, birthday, graduation, confirmation gifts all rolled into one slender package. Yet, even that doesn't quite describe it. My first fly rod, a real one—not borrowed or handed down—a genuine bamboo thing, was bought in the spring of 1956. With my own money. Sort of.

I was thirteen years old, working odd jobs—selling newspapers, refunding Coke bottles, working in the almond

The Fly Rod Chronicles

orchards, even picking up wind-blown walnuts along the highways to sell to Diamond Nut Company—anything to save enough money for that first rod.

Then I got lucky and found a part-time job at a local sporting goods store. I swept and mopped, carried out trash, stocked shelves, and answered the phone for Chet, the owner. After a while, he trusted me enough that he could leave me in charge while he went for lunch.

Until I got my own first fly rod, I had an old metal telescoping thing I found in the garage of one of the many rented houses where we lived when I was a kid. I found it stuck back behind the stacks of old *Life* and *Saturday Evening Post* magazines and the wobbly mountains of yellowing San Francisco Chronicles. I called it the "steel girder," but it was actually in pretty good condition, not rusted or bent. I don't think it had been used much. That was several years before my first *real* rod.

It was the year I turned nine, and we were new in the small mountain town of Feather Falls, California (the romantic name is deceptive), where my dad was starting his first teaching job. He contracted to teach fourth grade, which happened to be my grade; so, he was my teacher. Looking back, compared to all the teachers I've had in my entire schooling, here's how he stacked up: A good teacher, he had a keen interest in insects, rocks, plants and animals; so, we got a good dose of science instruction and some elementary ecology and conservation thrown in. Because of his enthusiasm, he got us excited about nature and science. We made gauze nets and cyanide killing

First Fly Rod

jars (unthinkable today) to collect insect specimens. We collected and identified rocks, leaves, and wildflowers.

We also got a good dose of early California history, complete with a model mission and pueblo we made out of miniature adobe bricks. We had a thriving adobe brick factory.

Native Americans fascinated me; they seemed to lead a cool life hunting and fishing and living off the land. There was a Native American kid in my class; he was quiet, but smart. His name was Skip Burdick. I guess because I was new and he was shy, we found something in common; we soon became good friends.

I was happy when Skip invited me for a sleepover at his house. The Burdick clan lived out in the woods at the end of a logging road that wound its way for a mile or so along a small, clear, sandy-bottomed creek known by the locals as Branch Ravine. Feather Falls was a logging town, a company-owned town. Most of the few hundred citizens either worked for the logging company or for the handful of services that supported the company's operations, including the gas station, school, and the small one-doctor clinic. There was also a big company store.

Mr. Burdick was one of a few independent loggers—"gyppos" they were called—who owned outright or leased their logging trucks and tractors from the company. These independents logged mostly on Forest Service-permitted forests, then sold their logs to the company. Mr. Burdick was a gyppo and proud of it. Nobody owned him; he could brag

The Fly Rod Chronicles

about owning his own truck and Caterpillar tractor. Skip's two older brothers worked for their dad. Some day, Skip said, when he was big enough (not *old,* but *big* enough) he was going to quit school and join his brothers in working for Mr. Burdick. That plan appealed to me, too.

One day, my dad asked about Branch Ravine in the sporting goods section of the company store. The manager of that department said there were a few small rainbows—natives, not planters—and a heckuva lot of salamanders. That's why nobody fished it. Nobody, that is, except Skip Burdick. And me.

Skip knew his home water; you could almost step off the back porch of their rough-cut board house into Branch Ravine. He also knew where the fish were and how to fish them. The sleepover promised to be a lesson in trout fishing. I sorely wanted to learn how to catch those Branch Ravine trout.

The summer before we moved to Feather Falls, we'd spent a few weeks up in Susanville, where Dad earned summer cash bossing a crew of hay balers on a big ranch. A few evenings, he took me out to a place in the high desert sage country where a small spring creek called Crystal Creek wandered through a couple miles of sand and sage before it dumped into a pretty, man-made lake.

We caught grasshoppers and drifted them back under the banks with Dad's new Eagle Claw fiber glass rod on big #2 hooks. Dad explained we needed the big #2 hooks to match the hook size to the lip size of the fish. The small trout, who acted more aggressive and hungry, would always race out first

First Fly Rod

to get the hoppers. When they couldn't get the thing in their tiny mouths because of the large hook size, there was just enough drift time, a few more seconds, for the bigger trout to take the bait. The larger hook also kept any smaller fish from swallowing the bait and having to be killed getting the hook out. I didn't know it, but we were practicing a primitive form of catch and release.

This technique produced enough fish in the ten- to thirteen-inch class to make a decent fish fry. My first trout was a ten-inch beauty, and I'll never forget how it happened: After the smaller "pickles" had a go at the hopper and failed, the line drifted for a couple more feet then stopped.

"Set it!" Dad yelled.

I looked at him blankly.

"Pull him in!" he instructed.

So, I gave the glass rod a mighty heave and the trout ended up in the sage about twenty feet behind me. Ever since, this technique of landing fish has been known in our family as "sage brushing."

"Careful of snakes," Dad warned, as I set out to retrieve my catch.

I found the fish flopping around in the sand under a sage bush next to some wild blue lupines. He was covered with sticks and dirt; I didn't care. He was my first trout; I had finally graduated from the baby bluegill farm ponds I had fished with willow poles and cork bobbers. I was a trout fisherman!

I hugged the trout to me; I didn't want to lose this one. I must have returned grinning; Dad was grinning, I know. Since we didn't have a camera, we dispensed with trophy pictures. Dad showed me how to smack it on the head with a rock to kill it quickly. I held it, feeling it quiver, then relax, the life quickly draining away. *So this is dying*, I thought. I can still remember the sadness that swept over me; I still experience that same old letdown whenever I hook a fish deep in its throat and can't get the hook out or cut the leader fast enough and the thing dies, blood streaming out its gills.

Dad, ever the science teacher, helped me examine my first trout closely. It was a dark green-backed, silver-sided, native rainbow. Its black specks were small but uniformly spread, like black pepper on a freshly cooked ear of corn. It was just on the verge of losing its parr markings. Dad pointed them out to me and said that is the mark of a true native trout. Its pinkish red stripe went from its gill covers clear down to the tail, passing in strong relief over the faint parr marks.

#

The old, metal telescoping rod I found in the garage was nine feet long. I bought a secondhand Perrine reel from Junky George's Thrift Store. The pearl retrieve handle had broken away, so I wrapped the little metal bolt with several winds of black electrical tape. It wasn't pretty, but it worked for me. I wasn't into aesthetics, neither was Skip Burdick. We were into catching and killing trout. The more the better! Hook 'em and cook 'em!

I bought a double taper oiled silk line from the closeout

First Fly Rod

table at the company store. For that, I had to spend fifty cents of the two dollars Grandpa Robertson sent me for my birthday in September. Hooks, leader, and sinkers cost another fifty cents. I invested some of my capital in a mail-order sales scheme advertised in the back of a Marvel comic book. I didn't recover my investment, but the family had a lot of pretty tins of clover-scented hand balm. Another ten cents bought a block of four new-issue, first-class stamps my dad and I were collecting. The rest of my money bought bubblegum with baseball trading cards, including a guy named Mickey Mantle who played for the Yankees, the team I hated at the time. I was a Dodger fan, thanks to my hero, Roy Campanella, who I wanted to be like because I was also a catcher. (I later switched loyalties to Nellie Fox of the Chicago White Sox. But that's another story.)

That outfit and I (with Skip Burdick's help) caught many trout from Branch Ravine. We also fished another brown trout stream, a spring creek that wandered through the only farm in the area. It was called Berry Creek, where, again using a #2 hook with a hopper, I caught my first brown, a fall-spawning female of around fourteen inches, full of eggs. Again, there was the sadness at the kill. But I spent many happy hours on those streams.

The time came when Dad got another teaching job, and we moved away from Feather Falls. While stuff was being loaded into the moving truck, my metal telescoper got smashed; I looked at it numbly, then threw it away.

That was a sign, an omen of some sort, that it was time.

The Fly Rod Chronicles

I had been preparing for three years to move up to a real fly rod. This was to be no ordinary rod. I wanted one like my other fishing buddy, Ron Salisbury, had. He had a nine-foot, three-piece bamboo Montague, with a cloth sack and an extra tip. A sexy golden beauty.

Chet must have read my mind. In 1956, bamboo rods were sort of phasing out of the fly-fishing scene in favor of the new technology: fiberglass. Chet had just the rod I wanted: a Montague Rapidan model, eight and a half foot, three sections with its own cloth bag and extra tip. This one even had its own tube; something I didn't know existed until then. I must have taken that rod down a hundred times to heft it, stroke it, waggle it and try some primitive false casting. Chet laughed and told me I was wearing out his inventory; nobody wanted to buy a used rod, and he'd end up having to mark it down in price. That was sweet music to my ears.

I think it was priced around twenty dollars. I didn't have that kind of capital to invest. I needed money to buy a bike so I could get a paper route to make more money to buy that sweet little Belgian-made 20-gauge double in his used guns rack.

But I also wanted that Montague. Badly. I lusted after it like nothing else. I fantasized about it more than about the girl next door. That rod was beyond beautiful. It had a darker shade of bamboo than anything I'd ever seen, a dark honey color. Chet said it was impregnated. I thought he was making a crude sexual joke. It gleamed in the light; the red silk windings were perfect. The nickel-silver guides, reel rings, and ferrules shone. I admired the craft and the craftsman behind this little

First Fly Rod

work of art. It had a fly keeper, a little ring just above the cork handle, cleverly tied onto the butt section, also wound with red silk. *How did they get bamboo shaped in a perfect hexagon?* I wondered. The discreet red and gold decal label, just above the handle, proudly announced that this was, in fact, a Montague Rapidan.

Finally, I screwed up the courage to ask Chet if he would sell me that rod—*the rod*—on the installment plan. I would work it off, only, "Can I please have it now to get in some last fall fishing before the season closed?" I begged.

He said he'd think about it over the weekend.

That weekend was agony. It was the only time I felt lucky that it was cold and rainy; I didn't feel bad being deprived of time on the stream. Monday finally came. School dragged that day. At last, the final bell rang and I ran for the bus. I got off four stops early, the one closest to Chet's shop. My steps slowed down as I entered the shop and approached the man.

Chet was busy with a customer, and I knew customers always came first. I busied myself dusting and straightening up some boxes of shotgun shells and deer rifle cartridges just to impress Chet with my hustle and concern about his store. Finally the guy left and Chet buried his face in a newspaper. I hung around the front counter, waiting.

Finally, after what seemed like an hour, Chet, put down the newspaper and took a sheet of paper out of the drawer under the counter, the one where he kept a loaded .44 magnum. He handed it across to me.

"Read it and, if you agree, we have a deal."

The Fly Rod Chronicles

I didn't need a lawyer to interpret this contract for me. It was pretty plain and simple: I owned the rod and Chet owned me at the rate of half my fifty-cents-an-hour wages until paid in full. I signed, he signed, we shook hands, and the Montague was my rod forever.

CHAPTER 3

It Always Rains On My Day Off

Weathermen are charlatans. It's a Friday morning in November. For the past several days I've been faithfully watching the weather reports on television and listening to the radio for good news. We got an early snowfall the end of October. It's now after the middle of November, with more snow threatening. Some of the ski resorts have opened early.

Conditions seem to be coming together for a blue wing

olive hatch or two, what with several balmy 55-degree days, cool nights, and more storms on the horizon.

Weathermen are guessers. The chirpy blondes and the slick-talking weather guys with the sparkling white teeth had been predicting snow for, get this, *late Friday afternoon or early Saturday morning.* Right. I'd been planning carefully for several days so I could take today—Friday—off to fish in the late afternoon, right when they were claiming it was going to snow.

On last night's Thursday evening news, the same forecast was repeated. After the news, I suggested to Janet—aka SWAMBO (She Who Always Must Be Obeyed)—that I needed to use her Jeep Cherokee today.

"What for?" she wanted to know.

I fibbed and made up some lame errands I needed to run, including getting a flu shot. She gave me that squinty-eyed look that says, "I call B.S." I think she suspected something fishy (literally).

"Use Drew's," she said.

That's my son's dilapidated Mazda. Drew's has nearly bald tires. With snow threatening, I didn't want to get trapped up the canyon faced with snowy roads for my return trip down. All I could do was hope and pray that the snow would hold off for a few more hours.

Not that I mind rainy or snowy conditions. Some of my best fishing has been in bad weather. I recall a pair of large trout I caught once in early April out on the Strawberry Reservoir, a huge cutthroat and a monster rainbow. I was

It Always Rains On My Day Off

returning from an early-morning court appearance on a case I had to try in Vernal in eastern Utah. It was late afternoon; it had been raining mixed with slushy snow off and on all day. Just by chance, I had my rod with me. (Truthfully, I always have my fly rod with me.)

As I approached the reservoir on U.S. 40 from the east, and around the last bend, a small shaft of sunlight was struggling through the low, heavy clouds. The clouds lifted and the rain slowed to a light drizzle as I pulled into a wide turnout area and parked. I sat there still dressed in my courtroom-proper business suit wondering if I should risk a dry cleaning bill for a couple of moments of stolen pleasure.

Pleasure won out. I strung up the rod and walked the hundred yards down to the inlet nearest the car park. There was one lone fisherman in a boat about a quarter of a mile offshore, hunched down in his poncho, trolling through the chop.

I saw a large swirl on the surface in close. I cast toward it, letting the plastic night crawler sink. It took about three seconds before the water erupted and I was firmly hooked onto the biggest fish I had ever caught on an artificial lure.

I played it for several minutes. It jumped once or twice, then tired, swimming ever closer in smaller and smaller lazy circles. I hadn't noticed, but the rain, mixed with big wet snowflakes, had started up again. My suit was soaked, as were my expensive wing tips; my Brooks Brothers tie was ruined, but I didn't care.

As I beached this five-pound monster rainbow, its mouth

gaped open and handfuls of freshwater snails spilled out. Even as I released it, the trout was snapping and gulping down on the escaping snails!

I cast out again, the rain and snow coming down even harder. I was soon into the rainbow's smaller cousin, a four-pound cutthroat. This hog had also gorged on snails!

I also recall many other days in similar conditions: salmon in Alaska; steelhead in Northern California; Dolly Varden and sea-run cutthroat in British Columbia. And browns on the Provo the day after Thanksgiving one year, where a four-pounder fell for a pink glo-bug with a red San Juan worm dropper.

#

Weathermen are entertainers. I tuned in the radio weather report at six-thirty this morning while Janet was getting ready for school. The bubbly weather girl reported snow was beginning to fall in Davis County (about twenty-five miles to the north). That meant that my timetable for the Friday get-away had accelerated by about eight hours. Panic began to set in. I could use my son's bald-tired car all right; but what if it started snowing and I got stuck up Big Cottonwood canyon? SWAMBO would kill me.

I should pause here to offer a note of explanation. She Who Always Must Be Obeyed was raised in a family of all girls; mine was all boys. I was raised on fishing and hunting; she was raised on university lectures and classical music.

It Always Rains On My Day Off

Here's how we have resolved our difference on the issue of Time Spent Fishing—Beneficial to Society, or a Major Waste of Time? We have a deal: For every hour I spend fishing, I agree to spend an hour doing chores around the house or yard. (Caution: Before any of you guys make the same deal with your spouse, check the fine print. In my contract, I'm charged with travel time to and from the fishing spots; *she* should have been the lawyer.)

But I digress: My plan had been to take my new rod out and give it a shakedown test on the ever-accommodating (and abundant) brookies in Big Cottonwood. Maybe even an errant brown or rainbow was possible. The new rod is a sweet, six-foot ten-inch split cane, blanks made by Jeff Fultz, and built out by my friend, Leo deMonbreun.

So far I had only been able to perform some backyard casting. It's beautiful: a honey-colored jewel, light in the hand, medium-fast action wrapped with amber silks. I guessed it at just around three and a half ounces. Leo said it was either a three- or four-weight, but I found the weight-forward four-weight worked best; perfect for quick loading at short distances. I also want to try it with a double taper three-weight some day.

This temptress was hiding in my fishing closet, out of sight. But I knew she was there, close by, constantly whispering, "Take me, take me." I was getting crazy with no fishing so far this month, and just six days away from Thanksgiving.

On January 1 of this past year, along with the normal, well-intentioned resolutions, I had put down on paper: "Fish forty times this year while proving to myself that it's possible to fish every month of the year." Therefore, I had bought my license about January 2 or 3, hoping to get my money's worth this time. So far, being only true to this one resolution and forsaking all the others, I've been fishing right on schedule. Except for November, and Friday was to be the day.

Thursday afternoon I had thought about what might be the best flies in these bad-weather-threatening conditions. Blue Wing Olive? Maybe. Tiny parachute Adams? Perhaps. Midges? Very likely. I looked through my fly boxes and determined I was well-stocked with Blue Wing Olives (BWOs) and Adamses, but dangerously low on midge patterns. I trekked to the fly shop, full of hope and confidence to stock up on some more flies.

At seven a.m., as my wife was leaving to teach her high school students the finer points of French reflexive verbs, the phone rang: one of my daughters calling to know if I could watch her six-year old. She had forgotten he was out of school today.

"Sure; bring him over," was all I could say.

I walked out to get the morning paper; a light rain was now falling. The temperature was dropping. So were my spirits.

I took the new rod out of its case, put it together and sadly waggled it a couple times. Putting it away, I thought back on how many other times in my life I had been rained out. Somehow we survive rainy days, don't we? I looked out the window of my office; the first few scattered flakes were falling. It was now eight-thirty.

It Always Rains On My Day Off

I tried to see The Big Picture: my wife comes from a long line of Idaho dry farmers. If anyone has a right to complain about the capricious Weather Gods, it should be the farmers of this country. They probably complain when there's not enough moisture, or too much. They complain when it's too cold, or too hot. Can it ever be ideal enough to please everyone?

And here I sit, selfishly complaining about the weather ruining my plans for a couple of hours of therapy; much-needed relief from the stresses of business and commerce. The planning and scheming had been delicious. Instead of selfishly whining, I tell myself, I should be glad I'm lucky enough to be self-employed; that I have the freedom to be available to help out my daughter, a single mom who never gets a break from parenting.

Really, why should I resent that I get to spend a few hours with my fatherless grandson? He is a bright lad, with a healthy curiosity about nature. He showed me a Web site with interactive frog dissection exercises. It's called Frog-guts. com. I love it!

I'll show him my fly-fishing photo album. I'll get out my fly boxes and explain what each pattern is and what it's supposed to imitate. I'll tell him some of my glory stories about fly fishing, and some memories of times spent with good friends or my kids in some of the greatest spots God ever created.

And someday, when he's old enough, I'll take him out and teach him how to cast a fly rod. I'll take him up to the Provo, or Idaho's South Fork, or with float tubes on Brighton's little

The Fly Rod Chronicles

jewel-like Silver Lake. And we'll actually use those flies in my box. And we'll be lucky and the fish will be rising and we'll catch a ton. And we'll scratch and play the "pull-my-finger" game, and tell jokes and eat convenience store junk food, the stuff SWAMBO and his mother frown upon.

And we'll generally do what boys do when they're out having clean, harmless fun.

And on the way back, he can drive the Cherokee and listen to rock music while I snooze.

But today, I'll be grateful for the water. We've been in drought conditions for several years now. This moisture was badly needed. If I want to fly fish, and I certainly do, there has to be water. To get water for the best fishing conditions, it has to rain and snow—a lot—between now and next spring. Even so...

Weathermen are scapegoats. I know what I'll do. I'll shift the blame for my foul mood to those witless weather wonks. And I'll find some comfort with the self-promise of There'll Be Another Day Soon. Maybe the day after Thanksgiving? And maybe that same big brown will be fooled by a pink glo bug. Yet another time....

Maybe...

CHAPTER 4

January 6

I must be crazy. What was I thinking? I'm sitting here with the car heater blasting, trying to thaw out my frozen hands and feet. It's January 6, and I'm parked beside a pretty trout stream in southern Utah. Officially I'm on my way to Las Vegas—on business.

The stream is one that doesn't get a lot of attention in national fly-fishing magazines or in the local press either. I like that. It's near a sleepy little town originally settled by Mormon pioneers in the mid-1800s. My son-in-law, Jeremy, has an ancestor, Duckworth Grimshaw (I like that name, sort of trips off the tongue), who was one of the original settlers.

Winter fly fishing: It's one of those things that seemed like a good idea at the time—buy your fishing license early in the year, find some open water in a relatively warm place (like southern Utah), and fish. Simple enough plan.

I've read numerous articles in fly-fishing magazines about the glories and advantages of winter fly fishing: hungry fish, bigger trout, stream all to yourself, etc. Of course, being the responsible writers the authors of such articles appear to be, they always throw in a footnote of caution. Dress warmly, be careful in the ice and snow, be extra careful wading, let someone know where you're going, etc. My son, Mark, and several fly-fishing friends have encouraged me to try it. Okay.

Second objective: Try out a new rod a friend recommended for small streams—a six-and-a-half foot, two-piece, three-weight graphite. Rigged up with an old, Orvis Battenkill reel, my lightest one, it seemed like an ideal small-stream setup.

The weather report was forecasting rain and snow. For several days a big storm down in the Gulf of Mexico had threatened to blow north. This was unusual for this time of year; most of the storms from the Gulf come during the monsoon months of August and September. This one looked like a runaway freight train-type of storm. *Doesn't bother me, I thought. Bring it on. All the better for BWOs and midges.*

January 6

Not being too familiar with this stream, I drove around for awhile, looking for a likely spot that was easy to access through the two-foot drifts piling up on the stream banks. I found what I was looking for and parked in a convenient turn out. It was around ten o'clock in the morning. There was a moderate wind, not too blustery, a few fat flakes of errant snow angled down now and then. A weak sun tried to bust through low scudding clouds.

It took me several minutes to work up the courage to leave my warm car. A few minutes later, I struggled into my waders and boots. Then, I spent a few minutes more to get the new rod strung up. I false cast a couple of times; the new rod seemed bottom heavy, even with my smallest, lightest reel.

Needing to know if there was any sort of a hatch going on, I peered over the edge of the snow banks, scanning the stream below. No bugs were coming off the water or in the air, unless there were some Snow Flies mixed in with the swirling snowflakes, which I doubted.

By now my fingers had numbed, even with my fleece, fingerless gloves on. I wasn't sure I could rig up a nymph outfit now, so I just opted to tie on a BWO midge and see if there were any takers. Easily said, but it took over ten minutes to tie the blasted #20 fly onto a 7x tippet, even with the aid of a fly threader, that device with a thin wire loop you poke through the tiny eyes of tiny hooks. It's a lot like the old needle threaders your grandmother used.

The smart guys who write about these things in the fly-fishing magazines highly recommend layering your clothing to keep warm. So I did: thermals, tee shirt, sweatshirt, with another layer of a pullover fleece jacket. Talk about a cocoon! Over that, I pulled on my Gore-Tex wading jacket; gave my cap an extra tug; and, out of habit, locked the SUV. I felt kind of stupid; what car thief is going to be dumb enough to be out in this weather? *I'm the only dumb one*, I thought. Besides, I'd only be about fifty yards away at any time, and the car would be in full view. Yeah, I would be in full view of my car as I lay at the bottom of a crevasse in the snow drifts, rapidly freezing to death.

I waddled the fifty yards downstream and surveyed the situation. My first challenge was figuring how to get myself over the crusted snowdrifts and down a twenty-foot bank. It wasn't steep, but judging from the few exposed boulders I could see, I had to assume there were many more the size of Volkswagens buried under that snow pile.

The safest way down, it seemed, was to slide down on my butt, feet first. There was a neat, V-shaped groove that ended about two feet above a shallow side pool. I made it down without incident (i.e., without impaling myself on a buried rock).

Okay, I'm safely down, now how do I get back out when it's time?

I'd worry about that later.

I checked my equipment again: surprisingly, the line wasn't frozen. Yet. *Just wait until it gets wet,* I thought. I felt the hook point, gave it a quick rub on the whetstone, and daubed some gink on the fly. Ready.

January 6

Just upstream, above a couple of large boulders, lay a nice pool, deep on the upstream side, but flattening out over a shallow, sandy bottom on the downstream edge. There was a nice little falls sluicing down the face of some rocks that created a sweet riffle before the stream tumbled into this nearer pool.

I guessed there might be a trout or two lying safely under the overhanging rocks. And one of them might be tempted to dart out and grab a fly that fell from above, just to the left of where the falls became the riffle. If I were a trout, that's where I'd lie in wait.

I wanted to check the stream temperature, just out of curiosity. My stream thermometer was busted. *Did I do it just now, sliding down the snow bank or sometime earlier?* I wondered.

Then I did another really dumb thing; I dipped my hand into the creek to see how cold it was. Icy. *Around thirty-nine degrees*, I'd guess. My fingers instantly became totally numb, useless. *Gee, this is fun.*

I had on a nine-foot leader, and with six feet of line, I could stay back, my profile somewhat hidden. The fly miraculously hit the spot I wanted and a nice trout did indeed rush out to grab it. Plan A was working.

I'm frequently surprised by the suddenness of a small trout's attack. One thinks of winter as a time when fish are lethargic, not too active. That's not true all the time. Fish still have to eat to survive, especially in winter, when insect hatches are not so abundant; when cold-water temperatures slow down the natural activity of nymphs, scuds, and so on.

I set and pulled in a ten-inch brown; not particularly fat, but surprisingly large for this small stream. The colors were spectacular, set against the white snow and gray sky. *Funny, he didn't fight too hard. Conserving calories, or just resigned*?

I really didn't want to get my other hand wet, so I knelt down and used my hemostat to release the hook. A quick twist and he was free. He stayed suspended in the shallows a few seconds, his gills working. Then in a flash, he shot back under the protective falls, leaving a little swirl of mica flakes settling to the sandy bottom, sparkling in the thin light.

I moved upstream, tried a few more holes that looked promising, but the temperature was dropping, and so was more snow. I was fast losing courage, and that turkey sandwich and thermos of hot chocolate in the car were tempting right then. I just wanted to get warm.

On other streams like the Provo I've come across the remains of small fires on the banks. *Were they made in the winter by a fly fisherman, or perhaps two? Did they use the fire to get warm? To brew up a pot of coffee?* That sounded nice to me right now; I could just stick my frozen fingers into the boiling coffee and thaw them out fast. But, with appointments to keep, I had to be moving on down I-15, so I skipped the idea of a small fire. Anyway, I didn't have a lighter or any matches on me, and I didn't see a lot of dry wood nearby. I needed to get up the bank and out of this stream and get my car heater going. Even with poly socks layered over with heavy wool ones, my feet were now too numb to feel anything.

January 6

Conveniently, I found a sloping bank that was partly free of snow. I side-stepped up, digging in, using my boot-sole edges much like the edges of skis.

Once I made the top, I stopped to catch my breath and have a last look around. This was truly a nice spot and I was lucky to be there, keeping a promise to myself to do some winter fly fishing.

Well, now I have.

The Fly Rod Chronicles

CHAPTER 5

Band Of Brothers

Part I

When you associate the word "brotherhood" with fly fishing, you normally think of a worldwide fraternity. You know the type: well-worn cargo pants; ball cap, advertising some brand-name fishing-rod manufacturer, with a beat up favorite fly stuck somewhere in the crown (mine happens to be "Captain Zonker," of the Bull Trout- double fame); sun burnt, melanoma-looking tops of ears; shirts with lots of big pockets. They're the ones carrying their rods onto airplanes—not trusting those precious sticks to careless baggage handlers—arguing their way on board with rod cases that obviously exceed the posted overhead baggage bin limits.

"I am *not* a terrorist, and this is *not* a weapon of mass destruction" (except as unleashed on huge San Juan rainbows).

But, in this case, I'm talking about *brothers*. Blood brothers. My brothers. By today's standards I happen to have a *lot* of brothers: seven, if you count my half brother, Norman, which I do—there are no *half* brothers in our family.

Over the years my mom got a lot of sympathy.

"No girls?" people would ask.

Our one little sister died when she was four. As rowdy as we were then, some suspected we were the cause of that little girl's early demise. But I assure you, she died of natural causes: diphtheria. It was a tragedy for our family; there was never another girl to replace Martha. Our mom never got over it.

Ever since I left home several decades ago and moved to Utah to seek my fame and fortune (both of which elude me), we brothers have not been very close. It's hard when you're scattered all over the map like we are.

So it was ironic that it took our mother's passing, then Dad's a couple years later, to sort of bring us together in a fishing-centered reunion. Our first ever.

I don't recall whose idea it was; doesn't matter. The point is, we were getting together for one day to fish. The date was

Band Of Brothers – Part I

set for late June 2002. The venue: Idaho's South Fork, close to where the four youngest—or what we call the "lower half—" were raised after my folks moved from California in the late '60s to get away from something, I was never sure what.

Here's the cast of characters: me, at age 60, the second-born after Norman (who had pressing business and couldn't come). My occupation: reformed lawyer (I tell people I used to be a lawyer until God found out; I was so ashamed, I quit); now I'm an investment banker/trout bum. Residence: Salt Lake City, only four hours' drive from the South Fork.

Next was Bobby, age 58, county projects repair supervisor, Baltimore, Maryland; an avid bow and black powder hunter. I really envy Bobby, living next to the abundant Chesapeake Bay area: Stripers!

Next was Fred, age 55, owner of a home-remodeling business, Joliet, Illinois, now badly crippled by arthritis but fiercely insisting nobody cut him any slack; and Jim, 52, mortgage banker, Plainfield, Illinois. (Here we skip Paul, 50, secondary education testing administrator, El Paso, Texas. He didn't make this trip.) Elvan, 48, juvenile probation officer, Rigby, Idaho, was next. He's the soft-spoken one of the family, which, in this noisy bunch, makes you lean in to hear what he has to say. Last was Joe, the "baby" of the family, age 45, and an elementary school principal, Atlanta, Georgia. He has honest-to-goodness movie-star-handsome looks.

Also included were the second generation, represented by my son, Mark, high school business teacher, Rigby; and Jim's son, Jonathon, Boulder, Colorado, nursing school student—

both gonzo fly fishermen.

We gathered to fish the famous salmon fly hatch; or, as the locals call them, "trout" flies. Mark had been following the hatch reports for several days, and things looked good. The bug hatch was moving progressively downstream.

Three driftboats had been arranged: one rented locally by Elvan, one owned by Mark and me, and one owned by Jim's brother-in-law, Brad Park.

We gathered early at the sportsmen's access, an excellent boat basin/ramp located on the South Fork at Hisie, east of Rigby.

It was joyous chaos as we met; we greeted each other with hugs, jokes, and the usual good-natured insults. Conditions could not have been more perfect: blue skies, moderate temperatures, and very little wind, which is a bonus on this broad river. Even in the parking lot, salmon flies fluttered around, the occasional one landing on us: a good sign.

Before starting out, we set the ground rules, wagered the usual bets: first fish, biggest fish, most, smallest, ugliest fish, etc. Flies only (no bait or spinners), much to the chagrin of the four boys from "back east."

"No fair! You guys fish here all the time!"

Whiners.

We strung up our rods and tied on the huge, bushy, salmon fly attractor patterns specially designed for this hatch. Mark and I had a couple dozen flies tied up by Steve Beck, full-hackled yet finished neat and pretty. It looked like we were ready to cast off and begin the float.

Band Of Brothers – Part I

We pulled on life vests, and that's when I discovered my wading belt was missing. I don't know how it came off; I thought I remembered putting it on earlier. It must have loosened when we were putting the boat in the water or something. Oh well, I'd just have to do without it this one time.

Fred went with Elvan in the rented boat. Jim and Bobby were with Jonathan in Brad's boat. I floated with Mark and Joe in our boat.

Within fifty yards from the boat ramp, we started getting action. Big hungry browns started smacking our huge salmon fly imitations. Joe made the first hookup and took "first fish" honors.

Bugs, big ones, were everywhere. It felt like the locust plague in ancient Egypt. Trout flies everywhere—flying, crawling, in our hair, our faces. At one time I was fascinated, watching over a dozen crawling on my rod; I had to shake them off to cast. Just for fun, I held out my artificial to see what would happen. Within seconds, a horny male jumped it. Yes, it was going to be a great, memorable day for sure.

The only downer was Elvan: It looked like he was struggling to control his boat. Strange. The river was fairly flat here, few curves; the current was smooth, too. But he was having a hard time anyway.

I went back to fishing, browns and cutts ripping out from shadows and cutbanks to attack the big flies in that slashing way when greed makes them lose all fear. I hooked a couple in the fifteen-inch range. Mark and Joe were hooking up, too.

The Fly Rod Chronicles

We missed a lot of strikes, snagged our flies on low-hanging branches and had to break them off. There's seldom any time to stop and retrieve a fly when you're drifting; that's why you use a short, heavy leader, no fine tippets here.

When someone gets a snag, you yell, "Duck!" Everyone ducks his head and hopes you don't get slapped in the scalp or back of the neck with a hook. The fly either pulls loose or breaks off. No time to stop and retrieve flies; you just repair the leader, tie on another fly and resume casting. I also know from past experience that a fishhook stuck in the thumb can be a huge distraction; it cuts into your fishing time.

We developed the "duck" rule one time after SWAMBO, Mark and I were on a late fall float on the South Fork, slapping big streamers in close to the banks. Mark was rowing; I was casting big streamers for spawning browns; Janet was stretched out in the stern, enjoying the sun on her face, taking a rare day off from teaching. I didn't warn her to duck when I was snagged up in a box elder tree. I jerked hard on the lead-head Clouser; it popped loose and stuck her in the cheek. Fortunately, the point only went in a little, not past the barb. It caused no permanent damage, only continuing embarrassment for me whenever she brings it up.

#

But, back to the Landerman Boys. Around noon, we stopped for lunch. Fred's wife, Sue, one of the best cooks around, had put up quite a lunch for us. We'd worked up a

Band Of Brothers – Part I

pretty good appetite and were looking forward to her ham sandwiches and all the trimmings. One thing the Landerman boys are all good at is eating. I remember a doughnut-eating contest I once had with my Grandpa Robertson. I barely lost, but he was at least twice my size back then.

We stopped on an island, about three acres in size, that had a sloping sandy beach where we pulled up the boats. It was warming up, so I dropped down my wader tops as the other guys were breaking out the lunch. I looked around and spotted a pod of nice-sized fish rising in the nearby side channel; I couldn't resist the temptation—*heck, I can eat later.* Rising fish don't wait; experience told me the rise could disappear just as fast as it came on.

"You going to eat?" someone asked, as I strolled away from the picnic in the direction of the risers.

"You guys go ahead. I want to check out the channel over there," I said.

I heard murmuring about my cheating to get "most fish" honors.

Whiners.

I false cast a few times, letting out line. It felt good to walk and stretch my legs after sitting in the back of the boat. I laid out a short cast to the nearest riser. I was fishing my old, familiar eight and a half foot, five-weight Fenwick HMG, the one Ben had given me to pay for his DUI legal fees many years back.

The fly drifted about six inches when the water erupted; a fat brown sucked it down—the sound was like a cow pulling

The Fly Rod Chronicles

a stuck leg out of the muck. I played it quickly; I was eager to cash in on the other hogs that were rising all around their hooked brother. I was amazed that fish can be so greedy when they're on a feeding frenzy—they didn't spook and the commotion didn't put them down. It didn't seem to faze them that the hooked brown and I were stirring up the water around them; they just kept on happily sucking down salmon flies all around the two of us—the hooked trout and me.

I brought the fish to the net, measured it (sixteen measured inches and a fat-three pounds, I guessed) and admired its butter-yellow belly, its many big, black and orange spots, with a few powder blue rings mixed in. He had actually swallowed the hook, so I had to be careful with the hemostat and then release him just as carefully.

As I dressed my fly and sharpened the hook for good measure, I was amused at the sucking, piggy noises the feeding trout were making all around me. I wouldn't have been surprised if one of them had actually squealed.

I cast again and was instantly hooked up to another fatty. I brought it in and released it back to the herd of hogs. Totally absorbed in the moment, I caught a couple more, all in the seventeen- to eighteen-inch class. It was feeding time and everybody wanted to get in on the action. I even caught a couple of big mountain whitefish (Rocky Mountain bonefish, as Mark calls them). I caught six fish and released them, without moving one step from where I started. That had to be top honors for "most fish" so far.

"Hey, Dick!"

Band Of Brothers – Part I

The call from the picnickers made me lose focus for an instant and I missed a strike. I tried to ignore them and concentrate on the big guy I had just missed. While I false cast a couple times, I looked over at the boats. They were loading up to leave.

"C'mon! Let's go!"

"Just one more!" I shouted back.

I had another strike, this time connecting with the biggest one of all so far. I horsed him hard with my 4x tippet; I was probably a little rougher releasing him than I should have been. No time to admire him up close, either. *Do they feel pain?* I wondered.

I hurried back to the beach. Mark and Jonathan were at the oars of their respective boats, shoving off. That left me with Elvan and Fred, which was okay. I hopped on board and offered to take the oars. Elvan shook his head; stubborn ex-Marine. I hungrily bit into a ham sandwich that Fred offered me.

I used to be in the Navy; I know something about boats and rowing. Up close I could see why Elvan was having trouble at the oars (all jokes about Marines aside).

The problem with this rented boat was that the oarsman's seat wasn't properly anchored; it slid back and forth with each stroke, so there was no effective leverage. Also, the oars were too long; the handles almost hit each other. Again I offered to row, but Elvan stuck to it. We didn't know it at the time, but we were just a few seconds away from disaster.

We went into a sharp S-curve that sort of straightened into

a broad pool with many conflicting currents. Coming out of the S-curve, Elvan was digging for leverage, but we were now drifting backwards. It all happened so fast. Suddenly, we were in deadly trouble.

We were out of control, rapidly sliding sideways towards a huge, half-submerged cottonwood tree lying across the channel. It was too late to correct and shoot one of the two channels on either side of the downed tree.

We smacked the tree hard, broadside. Then the laws of physics took over. The boat tipped sharply upstream, water poured in, and we were under in a second.

I think we all jumped clear, I'm not really sure. It was then, when icy water was pouring into the front of my open waders, that I remembered I had no wading belt on. Worse, after I finished my ham sandwich, I hadn't pulled the suspenders over my shoulders, nor had I put my lifejacket back on! I cursed my own stupidity.

I was now underwater, the boat upside down, directly over my head, blocking out the sun. I waited a few seconds, holding my breath until the stern cleared overhead and I could see sunlight above. I surfaced, gasping for breath, and grabbed at the stern rope trailing in the water.

I held on, trying to gain a grip on the boat like Elvan and Fred were doing. Fred didn't look too good; he was gripping the upturned boat as best he could with his crablike, arthritic hands. My feet bumped into some rocks as we started to slide over the front of a small gravelly falls toward a deeper pool. The gravel face was maybe fifteen feet long. I thought I might

Band Of Brothers – Part I

be able to pull us toward the near bank, only about ten feet away at that point. I heaved and the boat moved a couple feet toward the bank. I heaved a second time, but the bottom gave out from under me. I was suddenly in deep water again, sinking fast, my water-filled waders now pulling me under.

This sucks, I thought, as, exhausted, I let go of the painter, feeling myself literally drowning. I took a quick look at my situation: The nearest bank was about ten feet away, but I had to go through swifter water to get there, with no guarantee I'd make land before getting swept farther downstream. The other option was to try to swim to the bank on my left, more than fifteen feet away, in deeper but calmer water.

I opted for the left bank and tried to dogpaddle. No go. As I went under again, I had two thoughts: First, I regretted I wouldn't be able to see my newest grandson, Sam, who was being born that day in Salt Lake City.

Second, a thought from who knows where popped into my head; "Touch bottom!" a voice inside me said.

I took a deep breath and went down. My feet found bottom and I kicked as hard as I could, leaning hard to my left. I came up closer to shore. Filled with new energy and hope, I tried it a second time—and ended up closer still. Then, a third time. When I came up, my feet touched bottom and the water was below my chin.

I caught my breath, slogged to shore, and fell on my stomach, my legs still in the river. I lay there, my arms and legs trembling uncontrollably, gasping for air, my heart pounding dangerously fast.

The Fly Rod Chronicles

About then Mark and Joe came racing to me.

"Thank God!" Mark shouted. "Last I saw you; you were in really big trouble. We thought we were going to have to drag the river for a corpse."

"It's supposed to be the *Bow River* where I clock out," I said. (This in reference to a dream I once had in which I'm in my late 80s, floating the Bow River in Alberta. I hook into a monster brown who pulls me under. They find my corpse a few days later, a mile downstream, rod still in hand, dead brown still firmly hooked. But that's another story.)

They helped me pull off my waders; eyebrows rose when they saw how much water poured out.

After I had slid off, Elvan's rented boat apparently flipped again and sank about fifty yards downstream in a deep run. Luckily, Fred (arthritis and other infirmities notwithstanding) and Elvan were close to some large boulders. They hung on until some other fishermen rescued them. This was told me later; I never saw any of that happen.

I sat on the bank looking around, suddenly deeply appreciating the ability to breathe, feeling the warm sun drying my matted hair. I didn't see any gear floating or washed up anywhere. My Fenwick and old Battenkill reel were lost, along with two other spare rods and reels, several dozen flies, an Olympus camera, and other gear.

The downside was SWAMBO berating me for losing our camera; then my insurance agent informing me that if I'd been camping by the river and had the stuff *stolen*, I could have submitted a claim. Right…

Band Of Brothers – Part I

Mark asked me if I wanted to go home.

"Hell, no! I came here to fish, and we're wasting precious time standing around talking."

"He's okay," Joe said to Mark, laughing.

"Stuff it! And in case I forgot…thanks."

I had to swallow my pride and beg a loaner rod from Mark, but I caught another beautiful cutt on a red and yellow Clouser before the end of the float.

I took top honors for most fish. I'm still waiting for the five bucks.

But I did get the tee shirt.

The Fly Rod Chronicles

CHAPTER 6

What's the Point?
Part II

As I drove home after the encounter with the neighbor who asked me, "What's the point," I pondered. My confidence in fly fishing was a little shaken.

She had implied what I did for enjoyment, what I thought of as one of life's necessities, as therapy, as an escape to Nature, etc., was a waste of time, effort and resources. To be generous and give her every benefit, maybe she didn't *really* mean that. But at least that's how I took her meaning.

The Fly Rod Chronicles

The experience reminded me of an epic poem I read as an undergraduate in some English class long ago. It was called "The Watchers of the Skies," by a guy named Alfred Noyes.

The main character in *Watchers* is a young man, Tycho Brahe, who lived in Denmark in the 1500s. Tycho started out at the university studying law, then he got distracted. He fell in love with astronomy, star gazing, and the possibilities of learning the mysteries of the heavens. Not a very promising career, some would say.

As a very young man, he discovered a new star; the discovery brought him much fame at home and abroad.

Denmark had a king, Frederick, who encouraged learning, the arts and sciences. King Frederick became Tycho's patron. He bought Tycho a telescope and set him up with a tower, an observatory on a little island. Tycho named the place Uraniborg, the City of the Heavens. This was a secluded, happy place where he could look at the heavens at night. By day, Tycho would figure out his observations and chart what he discovered in some organized fashion. His work paid off and over the years, star by star was patiently set down by him with scientific precision.

This happy state continued for many years until one day King Frederick died and his son, Prince Christian, came to the throne. Christian was surrounded by a host of courtiers who made their living by stroking the king's ego.

Christian and his advisers knew about Tycho; they were also in an austerity mood. So the advisers were sent to visit Tycho and find out: Of what use is all the money we're

What's the Point? – Part II

spending on this "feckless" star gazing?

They asked Tycho what he had done with twenty-five years' worth of the king's money. He showed them his charts, over seven hundred stars all precisely laid out in their proper places.

"And is this all?" they asked.

"Not all, I hope," he said, "for I think before I die I shall have marked a thousand."

Then the laughter began.

"To what end the travail and the waste? Show its uses to us now, show them now before we go," demanded the condescending messengers.

In other words, what's the point?

# # #

As I write these words now, in the fall and winter of 2003-2004, I think of the many government and educational programs that have been cut in recent years, due to the same kind of thinking:

What's the point? Show us the value for today. Show us the cost efficiency. Show us why we shouldn't give tax money back to rich campaign contributors who don't really need the money.

We have no money available, so we kick unwed mothers off welfare benefits ("values").

Show us how *electives* in education (art, music, dance, theater, and so forth) will translate into higher test scores. (But, for crying out loud—don't cut back on sports programs!)

Show us why we shouldn't drill more oil and gas wells on public lands.

Show us why we should pay public teachers more, to keep their compensation competitive with industry.

Show us why we shouldn't spend billions invading Iraq on flimsy evidence and then award fat reconstruction contracts to our already wealthy friends who make huge campaign contributions to keep us in office.

"Show us, show us, show us!" the now-thinking pragmatists shout.

What we don't hear is the future benefit to our society if we spend more now on educating our children.

What we don't hear is a better way to deal with crime, rather than locking people up and throwing away the key.

What we don't hear is any discussion or open, honest debate about what will be the future costs to society if we continue cutting educational programs or locking people away for long prison terms without giving them any job skills for when they get out.

#

Back to Tycho. This was his answer, as found in the poem:

In the time to come, said Tycho Brahe,
Perhaps a hundred years, perhaps a thousand,
When our own poor names are quite forgotten,

What's the Point? – Part II

And our Kingdom's dust,
On one sure certain day, the torchbearers,
Will, at some point of contact, see a light
Moving upon this chaos. Though our eyes
Be shut forever in an iron sleep,
Their eyes shall see the Kingdom of the law,
Our undiscovered cosmos. They shall see it-
A new creation rising from the deep,
Beautiful, whole.
We are like men that hear
Disjointed notes of some supernal choir.
Year after year we patiently record
All we can gather. In that far off time
A people that we have not known shall hear them
Moving like music to a single end.

The messengers couldn't understand what Tycho was saying; couldn't, or wouldn't, understand. They reported back to the young King Christian. They said Tycho's work and dreams were valueless or, worse yet, dangerous, since any fruit they bore might fall in distant years to alien hands.

Tycho was sent away to exile. Uraniborg, the City of the Heavens, crumbled into the dust.

If you were Tycho, how would you respond to this tragic end to a dream? He went away declaring with hope that some day he would somehow still reach his goal of discovering a thousand stars. That way, in perhaps a hundred or even a thousand years, those who came after him, with their advanced knowledge and instruments, would be saved much

The Fly Rod Chronicles

time and effort and would more easily be able to achieve their goals. Tycho said that even though in the future he may be forgotten, those searchers of the skies in those far off times would receive the glory and the palms based on what he'd started, and he would be happy with that.

I admit that fly fishing is not as epic as was Tycho's passion.

I doubt there will be any legislation outlawing fly fishing anytime soon. There are many, many people, though, who do devote their entire lives to fly fishing: Ask my friend Clint Cameron, owner of Dolphins Resort in Campbell River, B.C., if there's a point to what he does 24/7/365. He owns and operates one of the finest fishing camps in all of North America, guiding hundreds of guests each year in pursuit of salmon, steelhead, and Bull Trout (Dolly Varden). Ask the same question to his dozen or so employees, the groundskeepers, guides, cooks, drivers, equipment repair people and so on.

And ask the thousands of fish and game wardens and biologists in this country, "What's the point of fly-fishing?"

Ask the residents of such towns as Ennis, Montana, where fly fishing is a very important part of the local economy, "What's the point?" Jobs, for one.

My passion may seem narrow, self-centered, and even snobbish and effete, compared to bigger world concerns. But I think, ultimately, there is a point to it.

We all face choices, every day of our lives. Some of us choose to engage in worthwhile things and others fritter away time, as Thoreau said, in trivialities. (This in connection with

What's the Point? – Part II

his famous, "simplify, simplify, simplify." Some have asked why not a single "simplify"?)

I'm sure there are many who think fly fishing is a trivial thing to pursue. I won't get into the merits of that debate. I can think of a lot of other things that *I* consider trivial. And to avoid ticking off a lot of people, or even whole industries, I wouldn't dare list them.

I've wondered what the world would be like if we didn't have fly fishing? What if suddenly it was done away with? What could take its place that would have the same enjoyment?

I remember something the writer Robert Ruark said in the Foreword to his novel *Something of Value:* "If a man does away with his traditional way of living and throws away his good customs, he had better first make certain that he has *something of valu*e to replace them." (*Basuto proverb)*

All I know about fly fishing is this: I like it a lot, it doesn't hurt anybody, not even the fish when we practice catch and release. It's a clean sport, it doesn't really hurt the environment, it manages to employ not a few people, and I probably won't be replacing it with anything else anytime soon that has any more value to me.

And next time my best answer to the question, "What's the point," (the one I feel most strongly, deep down inside) will be: Fly fishing happens to make me really *happy* when I'm absorbed in it.

I feel sorry for those who don't fly fish.

Those who don't, just don't get it.

The Fly Rod Chronicles

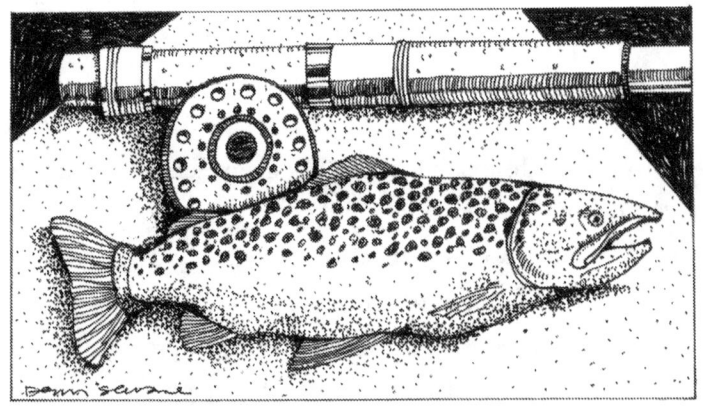

Chapter 7

You Never Have Any Fun

A few years ago, my son, Mark, was halfway through his undergraduate studies at Utah State University. We were discussing his major and what he thought he wanted to do in life.

He said, "I hope you're not disappointed, but I've switched from business to education: I've decided to become a teacher."

The Fly Rod Chronicles

For some time he had been talking about a major in business; the plan was that he would graduate, maybe even get an MBA, then come into my investment banking business, work his way up to partner, and, someday, take over the firm when I retired (or died, which was more likely to happen first).

I was not disappointed with his announcement. Truly. I give my children (and other folks, for that matter) a lot of latitude when it comes to their life's work. My wife and I are available to counsel, to be a resource, to help out financially and in other ways. But rarely would we ever presume to tell one of our children what we thought they ought or ought not to do. Only if they asked our honest opinion, and then only sparingly.

Anyway, I asked Mark in what field he thought he wanted to teach, and what had happened to bring this change. His answer was simple, brilliant and profound.

He said, "Yeah, I probably won't make much money as a teacher. But it's steady, it has good benefits, and I'll have my summers off to fly fish. Besides, I've watched you in your business. I'm not sure I want to work that hard. You work too hard, and *you never have any fun.*"

Meaning: You talk a good game, but you never really do get out fly fishing very much.

That was a few years ago.

True to his goals, Mark did his student teaching, graduated in both education and business communications, and searched for his first teaching job in a location that would give him

You Never Have Any Fun

optimum chances to fly fish—a lot.

He ended up in southern Idaho, in a nice little town called Rigby. He teaches at the high school, also does some coaching. He and his wife, Shiree; their two children, Skyler and Kenya; and their dog, Steve, live outside town, close to the Yellowstone Highway, just five minutes away from the famous South Fork of the Snake River.

His good friend also used to teach at Rigby High. Steve Beck loves the literature of Charles Dickens, is a world-class fly tier, and a brilliant fly-fisherman. Beck also happens to have a jet boat, one of those necessities if you want to fish the windy South Fork.

Mark has learned a lot from Beck, which he has then passed on to me. Steve has been gracious enough to take me along a couple of times, providing the boat, gas, lunch, his own flies, and some very sparing, soft, nonjudgmental advice on which of his beautifully tied patterns to use, where to cast, and how.

Mark, you're one of the luckiest guys in the world. Do you know how many guys in this country hate their situations and envy you green? How many of those poor guys would kill for what you have?

And talk about fun! Mark and Beck are out together year round an average of, I'd say, four times a month, more during their summer off from teaching. What's so bad about that life?

So, in the intervening five years or so since he made that comment, I have thought often about what he said, and I've since turned it from a pejorative into a positive invitation to live, to enjoy life, to suck the marrow. *Tempus fugit.* Time flies.

This obvious point was driven home forcefully last week when a friend's wife died suddenly; she was a year younger than my wife. My friend spoke about his wife at her funeral service. He spoke about what a big chunk had suddenly been ripped out of him. He tried to describe how lonely he was, how very much they had done together—drives in their vintage VW beetle convertible, cruises, etc.—how she had been his best friend and just how much he was going to miss her.

That caused me to think of my own life. I've dodged the Grim Reaper at least five different times (I won't go into all the details here). I'm still a few pounds overweight (working on it); I don't exercise enough (working on it); I eat too much of the wrong stuff (especially cheesecake, ice cream, smoked brats, pepperoni pizza, and nachos—working on it).

Like most modern American men, there's entirely too much stress in my life; i.e., I'm a workaholic and I overreact to a lot of trivial things that don't really matter much (such as ranting about feckless politicians and flipping off idiot drivers who run red lights).

And I don't dream, read, listen to Bach, watch baseball, call my kids/grandkids on the phone, play (translated: fly fish), or laugh often enough. That's the bad stuff.

But here's the good stuff: I'm a very lucky man. I have been blessed with a loving, devoted wife, six wonderful, talented,

You Never Have Any Fun

productive kids, and thirteen beautiful, clever grandchildren.

I have a fine education and meaningful, if not always financially rewarding, work. I'm my own boss; I can pretty much set my own hours. I have enough hobbies and talents to keep my life interesting. I live in a great community, close to some of the best fly fishing in the world. I have a nice home and beautiful yard, in a safe, clean neighborhood with friendly neighbors. I drive a decent car, and SWAMBO lets me use the Cherokee occasionally for my fishing trips. My beloved Utes actually won the conference championship *and* beat BYU. And I still have pretty good health.

But sitting in that chapel last week, listening to the words spoken at Linda's funeral, made me think a bit about my own future.

I suddenly pictured myself in twenty years; I saw an image like the Old Fisherman, the narrator, in the opening scene of Robert Redford's movie, *A River Runs Through It*. You know the one I'm talking about, where the camera shot is a close-up of the old man's hands. He's probably in his mid-eighties or so.

Those hands—the image of them—sweetly haunts me.

His hands are old, gnarled and bent with arthritis, scarred and mottled with age spots brought on by so much time in the sun and harsh Montana weather. He squints through reading glasses; he's struggling to tie on a *caddis* fly. His hands are shaking a bit, like older men's hands will do sometimes. It takes a while to finish the job.

That would be me in just twenty years!

The Fly Rod Chronicles

I know how fast twenty years goes by.

I well remember twenty years ago, plus: Memorial Day weekend, 1975, opening day of trout season. I took Mark, then not quite three years old, and his two older sisters, Amy and Heather, fishing up in the Heber Valley.

It was pouring rain when we left around eight o'clock that morning. I drove to where the highway crosses Daniel's Creek in Midway, near the state fish hatchery; because someone had suggested this would be an easy place to access for kid fishing. The rain had mostly stopped when we pulled off the road next to a small diversion dam that spills the water over into a large, dark pool. The creek then runs away into some farmer's pasture, first twisting gently under some big, ancient willows.

The girls were full of energy; it was obvious fishing couldn't hold their interest very long. They ran around, glad to be out of our old Volvo wagon, throwing rocks into the creek in spite of my pleas and caution about scaring the fish.

The day before, I had bought cheap, K-Mart, kid-sized spinning outfits for them. I proceeded to thread a fat night crawler onto Mark's hook as he watched. I showed him how to cast the bait into the pool, just under the foam where the water spilled over the little diversion dam. I handed him the rod and told him to hold it for a minute while I baited up his sisters' rods.

I no sooner turned around and had a crawler in my hand, when Mark said, "Dad, I'm stuck!"

I turned to look, and his rod tip was bent down and

You Never Have Any Fun

throbbing.

"Reel it in," I said.

He looked confused.

"Crank the handle."

"I can't; it's stuck."

I could tell he had a nice trout hooked.

"Want Dad to help?" I asked.

He nodded, so I helped him reel in a fat, sixteen-inch, two-pound brown.

I showed the kids how to kill it by smacking it on the head with a big stick (obviously, this was before catch and release became popular). It quivered its last; I felt the familiar sadness that comes with killing something so beautiful. Each child got to touch and hold it; we admired its unique spotting and coloration. Then I took out my knife to gut it.

"No!" Mark shrieked. He grabbed his fish and hugged it to his little two-year-old chest, staring at me, his chin stuck out defiantly. He wouldn't let go of his fish; he fell asleep hugging it all the way home.

Mark decided to name his catch "George." We froze it whole and kept it for many years in our freezer. Whenever someone new would come to visit, Mark would tug their sleeve and ask, "Do you want to see George?" Then he'd drag out the ever-shrinking, freeze-dried George for the stranger to admire.

Seems like only yesterday.

###

The Fly Rod Chronicles

Fast-forward to 1983, late July; there's the tail-end of a salmon fly hatch (the locals, I later learn, call them *trout flies*) and I'm floating the South Fork with one of my brothers and my dad. It's Dad's first time ever to go fly fishing; he casts to a spot I recommend. (Actually, I *had* seen a large brown cruising in some shallows; I don't think he ever saw it.) He makes a decent cast with the big, hairy attractor fly I tie on for him. The water explodes two seconds later; he hooks and plays a trophy-size brown, nearly having a coronary landing it. We take pictures and congratulate him generously. And, just for that brief moment, I know, so clearly, just how truly happy he is.

Seems like only yesterday.

Then pffft! Suddenly, its twenty years later: Dad's gone, so is Mom. My brothers are scattered around the country in far cities, and we don't get together very much any more.

My sons and daughters, who were just little kids fishing on Daniel's Creek a rainy day in 1975, are now grown up with their own college degrees, husbands/wives, homes, mortgages, car payments, credit cards, and babies and the usual stresses of adult life. I'm the white-haired grandpa now.

And I look down at my own hands. They're starting to get gnarled and spotted, and it's hard to thread that blasted 7x tippet into the eye of that dang little size 22 midge without those dang (where-did-I-put-them?) 3.5x magnifying granny glasses.

I wade more slowly, more carefully now, with a wading

You Never Have Any Fun

staff (wishing I had two). I don't mind asking my son or fishing partner to hold my hand when I cross the stream in the very deep, swift places.

I no longer count how many trout I catch or keep track of how big they are. I just appreciate the sweet escapes, the furloughs granted by SWAMBO, feeling the sun on my face, hearing the water music, watching a pair of bald eagles engaging in airborne foreplay; inhaling the incomparable fragrance of crushed ferns I walk through streamside.

I'm also secretly glad when my grown son offers to drive the three and a half hours *both ways* to the Green River and back so I can nap.

I am getting familiar with the *Word* again. I start thinking in terms of who's going to inherit the bamboo fly rods I love so much. Will any heirs appreciate the craftsmanship and how I patiently had to learn a casting stroke that's so different from that used with the newer, high-tech rods?

For numerous reasons young folks don't understand, I've learned to avoid convenience store burritos and hot dogs on these fishing trips.

So, Mark, in response to your concern about my not having enough fun, I've taken action. Here's what I'm doing:

First, I decided to become more of a student of the sport of fly fishing. I've observed you; Beck; my brother-in-law, Doug Dickey; my friends, Bill Ransom, Mike Bennett, Randy Simpson, Brad Chappell, Doug Wilhite and many others, and tried to learn what you guys do and how you do it so easily, effortlessly, and gracefully. I take and keep notes. And I'm collecting newspaper, catalog, and magazine articles about fly fishing. I'm getting a fairly fat file of clippings. I'm checking out library books. The latest is on fishing wet flies. That's a throwback to a former era of bamboo and silk lines, with gut leaders. Do you know what gut is?

Second, I've returned to the basics: casting, knots, equipment care, fly patterns, how to read streams, presentations, etc., a refresher course. I've been reading everything good about fly fishing I can get my hands on; I've checked out and watched videos from the county library, over and over again. I collect Alaska salmon and halibut fishing brochures and dream. I watch more outdoor programs on TV than I used to (it drives SWAMBO crazy). I'm amazed at all the things I'm learning and re-learning.

I ask more questions now. I stop other fly fishers on the river and ask them how they're doing, what fly pattern they're using. How, why, what's this, what's it for, what does it do, etc. I'm like a kid again, with a kid-like curiosity. I don't assume; I don't arrogate.

I take out my lovely bamboo fly rods as often as possible. I put them together, I feel their smooth surfaces, I admire them, I appreciate them as the tools they're meant to be. I waggle and cast them on the grass in the backyard. I'm even learning how to cast left-handed. You never know, in a few years I may be so crippled with arthritis in my right hand... The exercise keeps me familiar with my own rods, keeps my timing and stroke technique in tune, and helps keep the lines limber.

You Never Have Any Fun

Because of you, Mark, and your eagerness to try new things, I'm following your lead and branching out from just dry fly fishing. Why didn't I discover the joys of fishing with wets, nymphs, streamers, emergers, terrestrials, and midges, a long time ago? Just a traditionalist, I guess. It's a lot easier and more exciting to see a dry fly, to see the trout take the fly on the surface.

But now that I've practiced several times with each technique, I'm actually getting better, and it's providing a lot more zest to my fly fishing. This is especially true in mid-summer, when it's hot and slow or the trout aren't taking on the surface or there aren't any hatches going on. I've now found several new ways to make it happen.

Because of you, I tried float tube fishing for the first time this past summer. I can't get enough of it! Also, because of you, I discovered that fly fishing for small mouth bass on a light rod can be just as much or more fun than fishing for trout.

And Mark, you gave me confidence and taught me the basics of nymphs and streamers. You are in the right profession; you are a good teacher. I thank you for that. Maybe if I get good enough on wets and midges I can show you how, if you want. Then we can have a lot more fun…together.

The Fly Rod Chronicles

CHAPTER 8

Lemon Meringue Pie

It's two days before Thanksgiving, the weather has been unusually cold and I'm getting a serious case of cabin fever, what somebody once called "the shack nasties." Last night SWAMBO gave me the list of To Do's and stuff to buy at Costco. I saw a surfeit of sweets, starches and carbs. I saw a plethora of pies, but nothing really good, nothing I'd want to eat. I didn't see "Dick: fly fishing" on the To Do list, either.

"I don't see T-bone steak, prawns, baked potato with sour

cream and chives on this menu!," I shouted up the stairs, trying to be heard over the wicked Priest Frollo, singing loudly in French about his shameful lust for Esmeralda. "And I don't see any cashews...and where's the lemon meringue pie?" I demanded.

She never heard a word; Frollo drowned me out.

I don't much like turkey and all that goes with it. Pumpkin pie is okay with a cold glass of milk. My daughter, Amy the lawyer, makes killer caramelized onion gravy with garlic mashed potatoes that I like very much. Except for that and SWAMBO's Sara Salad, I could skip all the rest.

Frankly, I'm okay with a big bag of potato chips, plenty of cold diet Pepsi, and a big block of time with a buddy or two to watch the Detroit Lions in their traditional Thanksgiving Day game. They might even win this year. But I digress.

This is the time of year when tradition dictates being grateful for our blessings. Not that I'm ungrateful, but don't we overdo it a bit? Some of our neighbors (not in our cul-de-sac, thankfully, but down the street) were putting up outdoor Christmas lights (I'm not making this up) *two weeks ago*!

We're overwhelmed by *things*. We're drowning in *faux* prosperity. I agonize over the amount of stuff in my closet. I probably have eight or nine suits; I don't really know, maybe more. Like the rest of you, I can only wear one at a time, and that's normally on Sunday. I have about six or seven blazers and tweed sports coats with slacks; ditto the above. About four dozen shirts, half of which are the "dress" type, i.e., Sunday shirts. Not much use the other six days. About the

Lemon Meringue Pie

same number of neckties. Ditto.

I also looked in my fishing closet and took inventory of my fly rods and reels. I have about…well, anyway, that's not really important.

The other night SWAMBO and I were over at her mother's house visiting. She's eighty-eight years old, a widow, about five feet tall and maybe ninety pounds after a big meal. She tries to walk every day on her treadmill and takes care of a big house and yard. She has about all the creature comforts you could ask for. She's very high up in my Pantheon of heroes.

Her husband, my father-in-law, was a biochemist, graduated from Utah State; then got his PhD at Wisconsin. Then he went on to be a college professor at several Big Ten schools. They lived frugally, scrimping and saving for that proverbial rainy day. He invested wisely in safe and conservative ways: municipal bonds, pharmaceuticals, CDs, etc. She's pretty well off. But she doesn't have *him*. She misses *him* a lot; we do, too.

She told us how Lauren, one of my nieces, visited her recently to interview her about when she was young, what it was like growing up way back then, and so on. My mother-in-law was born and raised on a modest, dry-farming operation in the small town of Downey, in southeastern Idaho. Life was hard; there wasn't much cash circulating then. They learned how to survive and live off the products of their own labors. Farming was like that in those days, still is. It was even tougher during the Great Depression.

Her mother, my wife's Grandmother Criddle, who

The Fly Rod Chronicles

I adored (and who had the softest cheeks God ever gave a woman), traded eggs to a neighbor so her girls, including my mother-in-law, could have piano lessons. In my wife's home, growing up, music was an integral part of their life; music lessons were encouraged, provided, expected. The tradition continued with our children. I have two daughters who are great pianists, could have been on the concert circuit if they had chosen to be.

Maurine, my mother-in-law, told Lauren that she graduated from high school in the depths of the Depression. She wanted to go to college, but wasn't sure until the very last minute if there would even be any money for tuition, let alone room and board. On faith, she and her sister went to Logan, Utah, found a room to share and registered for college at Utah State University (or the "AC" as it was known back then; many people in Cache Valley, Utah, still call it by that name). They found part-time jobs and finally some money came through from home. Maurine later graduated from Utah State with her future husband.

Lauren was flabbergasted that Maurine's parents hadn't planned, hadn't set up a college fund when she was little.

"Didn't they want you to go to college?"

Lauren's generation just can't picture those conditions, the extreme poverty, hardship and want. They can't imagine no jobs, no cash circulating. Sure, some of them read Steinbeck's *Grapes of Wrath* in school. But they don't really believe it; it's just a story—after all, it's only fiction. They don't really *know* what it was like. They have no similar experiences, nothing

Lemon Meringue Pie

even remotely close to poverty to relate to in their day.

As I listened, I was reminded of a time when I was back in New York City with one of my partners, Bill Bodine, who lives and works there. Bill had set up a series of business meetings, "pitch" sessions, for our client over several days. This was pre-9/11.

A pitch session is where you go in and, as Bill describes it, you get one single opportunity to pitch your deal to these Major League investors to swing at. Our client was trying to raise a modest amount of capital, about five million dollars, I recall. We had met with several groups that represented "institutional" investors: large insurance companies, mutual funds, etc. In the financial community, these people are known as money managers. They look at financing proposals, analyze them, and make "yes" or "no" recommendations to their clients (most often it's "no").

Bill calls them "gatekeepers"—they guard the gates to the mythical fences that surround presumed huge mountains of investment capital. These are the gates for which we have to obtain a pass in order to enter and scoop up large wheelbarrow loads of money. Or so the theory goes.

I noticed that most of these money managers were quite young, relative to my age and Bill's. I guessed their average age was around (I'm not exaggerating) maybe twenty-seven. They were shiny and scrubbed and self-confident and newly graduated with their MBAs from Harvard, Amos Tuck, the Chicago School, Stanford, Wharton, etc. They were quite secure with their diplomas, large salaries, bonuses and perks.

I was amused, yet frustrated, as I listened to their turn-down speeches.

It became a familiar mantra: "We don't do deals under twenty million."

Those little snobs; what arrogance! Yet they did have a point. After all, they were making decisions affecting funds with billions of dollars under their management. There was a lot of pressure on them not to screw up.

Then I wondered how they would act in an economic downturn. Where were the guys with the gray hair and battle scars; the ones who had lived, worked and survived through the bad cycles as well as the prosperous ones? We were just coming off a decade of an ever-ascending stock market; it looked like there was no end in sight to this tech-stock-driven boom.

How would these *wunderkind* act and survive in a bad cycle, a bust, a Bear market?

We soon found out. It's only a couple of years later now, and Bill tells me most of these kids are now either unemployed, on welfare, or working minimum-wage jobs and glad to get enough just to pay rent and eat. Not that I take any joy in their misery. Millions of people worldwide are adversely affected when the economy sours.

The saddest part of this tale is that so many of these young people define who they *are* by what they *do*. Take away their means of doing and you take away who they are.

For example, if I graduate from law school, then society, my clients, the Bar, my family, friends, and neighbors, all

Lemon Meringue Pie

expect me to act in a certain way. I'm supposed to act *like a lawyer* acts, whatever that may be. But if I don't *act* in that way, they say, "Oh that's just not the *real* Richard, or Amy, or whoever." It becomes confusing to clients, judges, other lawyers, if I begin to act like a minister or a hairdresser in the conduct of my professional duties.

I suppose that's why a long time ago they set up professional standards of behavior, or canons. Canons were created to assure society that lawyers would always act predictably: like lawyers. Teachers would act predictably, like teachers. And so on, pick your profession.

What if you don't like your role? What if you are uncomfortable or unhappy in that role? A few hundred years ago, it was too bad for you. Today we have more options. We do have some freedom to choose to change things. That's one of the reasons I'm glad I live in the country I do, with the freedoms we have. That's a great blessing.

But what if the whole economy goes south and your job, your *role*, is taken away? Then, how will you define yourself? What do you have inside, deep down, to call upon? Will all your stuff, your car, your clothes, your degrees come to your rescue?

Speaking of stuff, I listened to a piece on National Public Radio (NPR) the other day. It was an essay by a young Vietnamese man on what it's like to have been born in Asia but to grow up in our culture. He described how in a Vietnamese family, everybody lived, ate, slept, bathed, dressed, etc., in very close proximity to one another—mom, dad, children,

The Fly Rod Chronicles

grandparents, uncles and aunts. He told of everyone in the family living close together, really close—telling stories, singing traditional songs, eating, laughing, touching, loving, and grieving—together in a community. He explained that grandparents, uncles, neighbors, all are aware of what children are doing, who they're doing it with, and are only too willing to share this intelligence with Mom and Dad—It's the old *it-takes-a-village* theory in action.

He soon found things are different here in America. At first, when Vietnamese families first come to America, they work and live together in crowded apartments, sometimes two or even three families sharing. Then they prosper by communal hard work and thrift. They begin to move out to bigger places. Just about everybody has his or her own room. They have their own space. Then they begin to acquire and accumulate their own things.

They quickly become *Americanized*: The kids grow up, graduate from college, leave home, get their own apartments, and get jobs in distant cities. They have their own space, their own stuff. Excuses are made for not coming home, for missing the family events. The coming together as a family, as a community, fades away, then dies. Something precious is lost in the process of finding one's own space.

But that's America. Is that what you really want? Is that what defines you?

A friend of mine once talked about living a "simple and provident" life. I've pondered that phrase many times, trying to understand its meaning. I've tried to envision what kind of

Lemon Meringue Pie

life that is. I think I have few ideas:

Do we really need such big houses?

Do we really need that many cars? Televisions, CD players, Gameboys?

Do we really need to buy new clothes every season of every year?

Is it necessary to eat out so often? Could we learn how to make menus, shop rationally, cook, and sit down and eat a meal together as a family?

Would it kill us if we didn't go on an expensive vacation trip every year?

Is it really necessary for us to mortgage the farm to finance college for our children in the most expensive, far-away schools? What's wrong with going to the "home town" university—University of Utah, or Utah State, or Weber State, or Cal State Fullerton, or whatever is close to home—getting good grades, a good education, and then earning scholarships for advanced studies?

Do we have to spend all of our leisure, discretionary time seeking for or being entertained? Is it possible to turn off the TV, take some scheduled time just to read, listen to classical music, go for a walk, say hello to a neighbor, volunteer for some community service? Would our favorite pro or college football program suffer if we missed a game now and then?

What would it do for our marriages if we spent just one hour a week listening to our spouse talk about her goals, her dreams, her hurts, her disappointments and frustrations or her successes?

The Fly Rod Chronicles

What if, instead of waiting to be asked, we volunteered to help within our church, work, school, family, community, or the local chapter of Trout Unlimited?

And what if we simply spent an hour now and then just thinking, pondering, praying, and listening to the sweet sounds of silence, or of nature?

What if we worked an hour or two less and played an hour or two more with our kids, grandkids, or with each other?

What if we took that extra hour now and then and devoted it to exercise or to a hobby?

Yeah, like fly fishing...

So, in keeping with the Thanksgiving spirit, I'm very grateful for fly fishing. What's that got to do with it? When things close in, when dealing with problems and people; when too much thinking overloads my brain like a clogged toilet drain, I go fly fishing.

Just one hour, I assure you, even on nearby Big Cottonwood Creek, even catching one, maybe two, eight-inch brookies—now that's a mental/psychological dose of Drano for my system.

Try it.

And please pass another slice of lemon meringue pie. Thank you.

Chapter 9

The Moustache Factor

I ran into an old friend the other day at the Orvis shop. I'll call him Don, since that's really his name. We were in the same small firm together when I first started practicing law many years ago. We were only together about two years before I left that firm and took another job as an administrative law judge for the state.

But while we worked in the same office, I came to like and appreciate Don very much. He was a country boy through and through. Why he became a lawyer is a mystery. But then I've found a lot of lawyers over the years who don't seem at all suited to the profession. Somebody somewhere must have told them, "Hey, you'd make a great lawyer!" and they believed it. I also know a lot of lawyers who hate what they do. I understand.

For example, early in my lawyer days we had a neighbor who specialized strictly in trial practice. He was a miserable, mean, ornery guy. The only thing that saved him as a human being was his saintly wife. Everybody loved her; they barely tolerated him

Why? Because, like most trial lawyers, he was always in a litigious mode. Just like actors who are always "on," his persona was constantly wired into a signal that said, "Fight, Fight, Fight! Win! Win! Win!"

I wondered whether he ever relaxed, laughed, told jokes, had any fun. Did he ever go fly fishing, or any other kind of fishing? Probably not.

Don was just the opposite. He was too nice to be a trial lawyer, though he spent a lot of time in court doing personal injury stuff and divorces that started out as "hand-holding" cases and suddenly turned really nasty along the way to a settlement.

A lot of Don's legal services became *pro bono*, not by design, but by default. Don had a hard time asking for fees.

The Moustache Factor

He did a lousy job doing collection work because of his compassion. He admitted he lacked steel, toughness.

Don's nemesis was a certain district court judge who, for obvious reasons (even though he has long since died), shall be given a fictitious name. Judge "Black" hated Don, and Don made no secret of how he despised Judge Black in return. Because I was the new man in the firm, Don often asked me to cover for him for hearings, motions, etc., before Judge Black.

Somehow Judge Black took pity on me, a greenhorn lawyer, and would hold my hand (metaphorically speaking) through some of *my* stumbling moments. He would ask where Don was, and why was I sent to "cover" for him? (his meaning being obvious). Don and I became very creative at making up new excuses.

I didn't mind. I liked Don. Very much. He sort of took me under his wing, nurtured me, showed me the ropes, and helped me weave my way through the landmine-field of office politics. I've never forgotten his kindness or his dry wit.

A certain other judge, whom I'm happy to name, took a liking to me. I became sort of a mascot to him, too. Judge Stew Hansen, Sr., was a crusty old curmudgeon but we loved his wit, his keen insights, and his fairness. He soon discovered that I was new to the law and that, prior to starting law practice, I had just recently returned home from a two-year tour as a Navy Reservist. He called me "lad," more as a term of endearment, I hoped, than as a putdown.

The moniker stuck at the office, and Don took to calling

me "lad" every chance he saw me; I didn't mind.

Don had piercing brown eyes that drilled right through you. He could cut through bull crap faster than anybody I've ever known. He also sported a moustache, which I thought was really cool. So I grew one, too. My motivation was to try to overcome the Boy-Next-Door image and look older. If *I* looked older, I reasoned, I'd get more respect at court and from clients. No more "lad" business. No sir.

I grew a beautiful moustache. I hoped Omar Sharif, the actor, would weep for shame when he saw mine. My moustache was full, florid, and red. That surprised me, until my Dad said my Grandpa Landerman (whom I never knew) had a red beard.

I left that firm after a year or so. They didn't pay me enough to support my young family and the mortgage on our first little home.

Those were the '70s and facial hair was cool; beards were in. But the '70s faded. Time passed. I shaved my moustache; I don't remember why, I just did.

I didn't see Don much after that; my practice took me away from court appearances. In fact, until I saw Don the other day, it had been about twenty years.

As I entered the Orvis shop that day, I noticed an older-looking man. He wore an Indiana Jones fishing fedora, and sported a sandy-red beard. I nodded as I passed him. He came up to me a few minutes later and spoke. Even though I didn't recognize the face at first, the voice was distinctive. It was Don. I was pleased to see him. We shook hands and hugged;

The Moustache Factor

we quickly caught up on each other and traded phone numbers, promising to go fishing together some time soon.

Later, I wondered how I would look now with a beard, or at least a moustache. My Dad never grew a moustache, although he did have a great beard his last year of college. He grew it as part of a Pioneer Days competition at Chico State College; he didn't win first place, but he did come in third. My uncle Arnold, with whom I fished and hunted as a boy, had a cool salt-and-pepper moustache. My mom's baby brother, Floyd Robertson, has had various forms of facial hair through the years. A lot of my friends have facial hair. What would it hurt if I grew a moustache again?

###

A few summers ago, I took Mark to Alaska salmon fishing. The evening we landed in Anchorage it was pouring rain, not a promising sign. My wife's sister and her husband, Jeanne and Doug Dickey, picked us up at the airport. Their beautiful home on a mountainside above Anchorage became our base camp. Next day, while we were getting licenses and stamps, flies, etc., the sky began to clear. Doug, who's fly fished a lot of Alaskan waters, was concerned that the river we'd be fishing would be way off-color.

There was no need for concern; as it turned out, we had a great three and a half days on the Talachulitna River, about forty minute's flying time west of Anchorage. We stayed at a nice little lodge run by some great people. This was in mid-

The Fly Rod Chronicles

August, the start of the run of the coho salmon—the fabled silvers. We only had a window of that one week; Mark had to get back home by Sunday to begin his school year the next day.

Two weeks before we went to Alaska, I did my annual trip to the dermatologist to have "pre-cancerous" age spots removed from my face. If you've never had this done, you're in for a treat. The doctor locates spots on your arms, back, chest, face, even in your scalp, and burns them off by applying liquid nitrogen. It's freezing cold at first. Then the burning starts. Not comfortable. Later your face looks like a bad, week-old pepperoni pizza. You look like you really do have cancer breaking out all over.

It hurts to shave; in fact, you shouldn't shave for a while after because shaving scrapes off the scabs and you don't want to risk infection. So, I had a convenient excuse to avoid the razor for awhile.

Actually, two excuses.

The second excuse: You don't really want to shave while in the Alaskan Bush. Obviously, you want to spend as much time fishing as possible. The days are long, the nights are short and every minute counts when you've spent that much money and traveled so far. Also, they have something up there called "no-see-ums," sort of blood-sucking midges, only smaller. Little nasty bugs, swarms of them; they come armed with "no-see-um" hypodermic needles as snouts. They have a stinging bite and bother you without mercy. They just *love* the scent of after-shave lotion. You don't want to leave any trail that's

The Moustache Factor

easy for these monsters to follow. Ditto that for bears.

We were pretty darn lucky about the bugs; we didn't really get bothered much. It had rained like the dickens for several days before we got there. When the Dickeys had picked us up at Anchorage International, Doug mentioned the weather was supposed to clear the next day. We hoped. Darn weathermen again.

When we got up the morning after arriving, the sky was heavy with big, fat, threatening rain clouds. It didn't look good.

###

We left Lake Hood in a small float plane around one o'clock, heading for our camp, flying just under the heavy cloud ceiling at about 1,500 feet. Mark sat in front while I tried to snooze in back, but the engine was too loud and I was too excited. I've been to Alaska numerous times, but this was the first time fly fishing for salmon. We were going to be there for the peak of the coho run, silvers. We hoped there would be a record run for us—but there was no guarantee—they can be moody that way.

Then I saw a big river below, milky-blue in color, fresh out of a glacier, a good sign. Our pilot throttled back, banked to the left, and in about sixty seconds we had dropped down just above the river. We skimmed the water, slowed, then smoothly slid over to a big sandbar where a flat power launch was beached and two men in waders stood by.

The Fly Rod Chronicles

Our ride to camp in the launch took us up the glacial river a short distance. Then we branched off to the left and we were on the Tal. In stark contrast to the milky-blue glacial river we had just landed on, the Tal was about the color of strong coffee with a good splash of cream thrown in. Our host, Dave, who had a splendid moustache, explained over the motor that, yes, the rain had recently been heavy, but he thought it would clear up soon enough. Shouldn't bother the fishing much, he thought. I hoped so. He said the party that had just left had all caught limits of silvers. I enjoyed the breeze pleasantly rustling in my fledgling beard.

We arrived at camp, one of the prettiest spots I'd ever seen. We walked up a trail from the boat ramp through thick fern stands higher than my head. I swore I could smell bear scat. We met Dave's wife, Claire, had a drink and snack, then stowed our extra stuff in our snug cabin. After a quick gourmet lunch, we met our guide, Matthew, and headed with our rods and fly boxes down to our boat. Matthew had a florid, scruffy red beard. Beards everywhere up here!

It's about a five-minute boat ride down river to the confluence where the Tal merges with the bigger glacial river. On the way down, we saw numerous bald eagles scavenging dead salmon washed up on gravel bars. Mark and I chattered about the ground rules and the bets.

On our fly-fishing outings, we like to bet—five bucks per category. The usual: First fish, most fish, biggest fish, smallest fish, ugliest fish, prettiest fish, and most original name for a fish. He almost always wins all but a few categories. (Except

The Moustache Factor

for the day after Thanksgiving a couple of years ago when I caught that big brown on the Provo with the pink glo bug dropped below a red San Juan worm; that was the first time I'd skunked Mark in about fifteen years.)

Within minutes we were anchored at the hole we would fish the next three days, and Mark and I both were tying on the flies Matthew recommended: egg-sucking leeches, size six. I started out with a black one "sucking" an orange egg. Mark tried an olive with a red egg. We were both using pretty heavy rods because that's what the literature said to do. I had my nine-foot Browning seven-weight rod. Mark's rod was the same weight.

We anchored about thirty to forty feet from the bank, opposite a moss-covered granite slab that rose twenty feet or so out of dark brown water. The rock was crowned by a pretty stand of dark evergreens and white-bark birches. We were casting across the current, snug up against the granite slab, using sinking tips, letting our big streamers drift downstream toward a shallower area that riffled over some submerged granite boulders. Matt thought the silvers were bunched up thickly just a few yards up from that spot, hugging the bank and stream bottom.

Mark cast first; his fly sank for about four or five seconds, then he let out a whoop when we both saw his line stop and pull away fast. He set the hook and was tight on a pretty, male coho. The line sliced through the water, throwing a rooster tail of spray, as the fish ran, then jumped, its sliver sides tinged with pink flashed in the sun. What a beautiful sight. Mark's reel sang; what a sweet sound. He won the first bet.

It was then I first noticed that the clouds had broken up; the sun was burning its way through. The light made the water look clearer.

Then it was my turn to holler, as my fly repeated the same performance. I was amazed at the strength of these fish. Mine also jumped; just like a rainbow, I thought. Matt took pictures of our first silvers. I'm hugging mine; my new beard was flourishing in these conditions.

We fished until our arms and backs ached, but we didn't care. This was the most fun we had ever had fly fishing. We stopped around seven for another gourmet dinner: roast beef, potatoes, vegetable, salad, and dessert. Then back out on the river until semi-dark, quitting time, which came around ten-thirty. Back to camp. I didn't even bother to shower; can't remember if I even got out of my clothes. We dropped, exhausted, into our beds that night. I slept like a spanked baby.

That first day was just a warm-up exercise. The next day was even better. Throughout that second day we lost count of how many we caught; I quit counting after about forty. I'm sure it was at least sixty for me. Mark probably caught three for every two I caught. And, we had sixteen "doubles"—sixteen times we each had salmon on at the same time that we actually brought to net.

We tried all kinds of patterns, mostly egg-sucking leeches of all colors: reds, purples, browns, orange, olives, with various combinations of egg colors. But, we found they went

The Moustache Factor

just as aggressively for Zonkers, Bunnies, Arctic Shrimp, Muddlers, and one killer fly Doug had tied up especially for salmon; I don't know what it's called. It's a skinny, purple thing with purple plastic "quill" wound around the shank, a collar of purple flash, and a tiny single spoon hanging off the hook's bend. It ought to be illegal, as the Bee Gees sang. They went nuts for that one. (As did the sea-run Bull Trout and cutts in B.C. last spring—another story.)

Guides talk to one another. They talk about their clients, whether they're good, bad, average; whether they'll be good tippers; whether they're doing well or having a miserable time; or, worse yet, whether they're giving everyone else in camp a miserable time. One thing I've learned about guides: If they're excessively polite, things aren't going well on the water. That wasn't the case with Matthew; he was a real professional and we had the time of our lives with his help.

A friend of Matthew's, a guide in the next camp up-river, had been complaining about one of his clients. It seems the guy was a jerk (well, he *was* a jerk, from what we saw firsthand); plus he couldn't cast a fly for spit. It was painfully obvious to anyone he should have stayed home; he just couldn't fish. We learned that this particular client had been complaining to Matt's friend all day that: a) there weren't any fish (although everyone else was catching fish and we were all so close together in our boats we sometimes had to reel in when another guy's fish ran toward us; b) even if there were fish, their boat was in the *wrong* spot and why didn't his guide move the boat to a better spot? (to which the guide tactfully explained that

The Fly Rod Chronicles

the spots were taken on a first-come-first-served basis; if you want a better spot don't stay up so late drinking and playing poker, and get out of bed earlier); c) his guide was choosing the wrong *flies* (no comment needed...well, I will comment: Any fly fisherman worth mentioning would come prepared with the right flies or at least some knowledge of what he needed from his guide, based on some advanced research); and d) his guide didn't know what he was *doing*! (Read on.)

In the evenings, after dinner, if the guest decides to stay in camp and not fish the evening bite, the guide gets to tie flies, goof off, fish if he wants, whatever. One thing I know about guides, they do what they do because they *love* to fly fish.

This guide was steamed; he just had to let off some pressure. What better way to prove the jerk was wrong on all counts, than by catching a few fish in the exact spot his client had hammered all day?

That second evening four of us—the maligned guide's partner, Mark, Matt and me—witnessed a clinic by that guide on fly casting: presenting the fly, hooking, playing, landing, and releasing fish; and on classy fly fishing in general.

Did I mention that Matt's guide friend had a moustache, too?

Every cast caught a silver. And with every beautiful, perfect cast, he made a comment about his "idiot, **hole" client and how he ought to be out here learning by watching instead of back in camp drinking himself senseless, etc., etc. Then he got bored.

I'm not making up what we saw next; Matt and Mark

The Moustache Factor

are my witnesses. This classy guide started making bets with himself. Picking up one of his client's cigarette butts from the boat's bottom; he tied it on a bare hook and said, "I'll bet I can catch one on this!"

He laid out a cast and was quickly tied onto an eight-pound coho. We laughed and cheered.

Then he found an apple core in the boat bottom and tied it onto his hook. Another cast, another fish. Again we laughed and cheered.

To top that, he found a piece of carrot stick left over from lunch.

"The carrot fly; a variation of the Bunny pattern!"

A perfect cast, this time backwards over his head, another hookup, another trophy. We laughed our guts out. It could have gone on like this, but dark was falling and we had to get back to camp.

A couple days later we said goodbye to Alaska, until another time. Before I left, I shaved off most of the facial hair that had accumulated. Except for the moustache. I left it alone.

When I got home, SWAMBO quickly spotted it.

"What's *that* thing?" she demanded. "It makes you look *old*."

(I must insert an editorial aside here: I don't think much of older guys who fight "it," who refuse to grow old gracefully. There's something patently ridiculous about older men— really *older* men—who leave their Hawaiian shirts open, wear gold bracelets, drench themselves in Aramis, do the "comb over," and use the Grecian Formula stuff; or, worse yet, who put on a really bad hairpiece. You can spot these guys across the parking lot, and I avoid them like the plague. I'm paranoid that their behavior is contagious. That Grecian stuff turns their hair a weird shade of orange or green. No thanks!)

Her words cut me. I swallowed my pride and bought some goo to paint in the moustache hair. It's supposed to match the original, natural color of your follicles. Or so the advertising promises. I can attest, it ain't necessarily so. It turned my brush a sort of brownish pinkish color—heavy on the pinkish side.

So, I did a strategic retreat. I got out the shaving cream and brush, lathered up, and shaved the whole thing off. She sort of smirked when she saw me shorn.

"Gracie [our granddaughter] complained when I tried to kiss her. She said it hurt," I explained.

"Oh," she smiled.

I refuse to let SWAMBO get the last laugh. In a few years, I'll be a bona fide old coot. Then I'll qualify for the real thing: a beautiful white moustache to go with my flowing white hair.

If I have any hair left by then.

Chapter 10

A Pretty Dry State

Utah is supposedly the first or second driest state in the nation. I'm referring here to water. Not a ranking to be proud of. We used to get a bad rap about our liquor laws, too, but I think the 2002 Winter Olympics changed a lot of that.

When I first moved to Utah in 1961, I was awed by the vast, open desert spaces, the dryness. Awed, that is, until I got out on a few weekends and saw the number of reservoirs, lakes, ponds, creeks, and rivers scattered around. Water everywhere, if you looked for it.

The Fly Rod Chronicles

Utah is home to a few Blue Ribbon rivers: most notably, the Provo and the Green. Both streams are jotted up by writers from all over the world. We don't have a lot of such fisheries, but those two, at least, put us on the map. Then there's the Weber, a decent trout stream. And we're within just a few hours' driving time from Wyoming and Idaho, with their great streams and lakes.

I mention the awe factor, because I came from Northern California where we seemed to have too much water. Is it possible out West to have too much water?

My hometown of Yuba City is bordered on the east by the Feather River, held in place by a system of levees. Just a few miles south of town, the Yuba River, flowing rapidly down from the Sierras, merges into the Feather.

About eighteen miles west of town is the Sacramento River, known all over for its abundant striper, salmon, shad, and steelhead fishing. The Feather merges into the Sacramento a few miles below where the Yuba merges into the Feather. Got that?

The Sacramento is then joined by the American River (another great salmon and steelhead fishing water) on the west side of Sacramento.

The Sacramento then flows on south for several miles, turns west at Stockton and merges with the San Joaquin, coming up from the south. Together, those two mighty rivers flow west a few miles and dump into the San Francisco Bay, where they become quite salty.

Got all that? If not, look at a map.

A Pretty Dry State

It flooded in Yuba City, badly, Christmas of 1955. The levees became water saturated and gave way, just a few hundred yards below where the Yuba River converges with the Feather. It was a result of several factors, especially an early snow pack in the Sierras that quickly melted due to some heavy, warm rainstorms in December. Result: Torrents of water came gushing down the mountains, looking for the low spots in the valley.

We had relatives and many friends who lived in Yuba City, so we spent some of our Christmas vacation helping with the cleanup efforts. We knew one family that got caught while trying to escape in their car. They all drowned.

A couple years later, we moved to Yuba City. The garage of our new home had several inches of silt left from the flood, atop the transverse 2x4 studs, about eight feet above ground. I still remember the rectangular spots on the ceiling of one house we cleaned; the rest of the ceiling was dirty. The rectangular spots were made by floating books.

In California, in addition to those famous rivers, there are many more sources of water. All through the nearby Sierras, you'll see any number of smaller creeks and streams that eventually find their way into the Sacramento, the Feather, or the Yuba. Streams with names like Berry Creek, Grizzly Creek, Granite Creek, Brush Creek, Big and Little Chico Creeks, and so on. Farther north there are the famous Hat Creek, Fall River, and the McCloud. On the coast are the Smith and the Trinity, known for their salmon and steelhead runs in summer.

The Fly Rod Chronicles

And of course, all these rivers, fed by the numerous streams and snow pack in December 1955, eventually flowed down through the Delta, merged with the San Joaquin coming up from the south, and it all dumped into San Francisco Bay.

From 1962 to 1964, I spent some time in British Columbia and Alaska. There's even more water in those places than California ever dreamed of. I managed to do quite a bit of trout and salmon fishing there, too.

At this point, someone is sure to quote Norman Maclean "…and a river runs through it." This is okay with me. Like all fly fisherpersons I, too, am haunted by waters.

I am amazed at the number of works of literature, art, and music that have *water* as the central theme.

Music: Handel's *Water Music,* Debussy's *La Mer,* Mendolssohn's *The Hebrides Overture,* Wagner and his Rhine music, *Die Moldau,* Respighi and his *Fountains of Rome.* Just to name a few. Even Ravel wrote a ditty about water and sunlight playing games with each other. Appropriately, he named it *Jeux d'Eau* (Water Games).

Literature: Hemingway's *Old Man and the Sea* and *Islands in the Stream.* The aforementioned Mr. Maclean. Kipling, Conrad, et al.

Art: Winslow Homer painted not a few canvases about the rugged New England coast, the sea, and the fishermen and sailors who tried to master it. And there's a nice canvas he painted of a pair of frolicking brook trout. One of my favorite paintings is a very haunting picture of the River Thames at sunset. As a bunch, the Impressionists were pretty darn good

A Pretty Dry State

at capturing the essence of water on their canvases. Monet painted over five dozen pictures of water and water lilies.

Back to literature. One of my favorite writers is John Steinbeck. I give you a bit of obscure literary history: Before Steinbeck became famous as a novelist, he wrote a little-known work called *The Log from the Sea of Cortez.* At first reading, this is a technical, scientific narrative of a year-long voyage Steinbeck took on the Sea of Cortez in an expeditionary ship of the same name. It was so named because the ship was fitted for scientific purposes, to explore, collect samples, and document the marine life in and around the Sea of Cortez, known to most people as the Gulf of California. The ship was literally a floating science laboratory.

Among his other duties, Steinbeck faithfully kept the ship's log, noting such boring nautical items as locations in latitude, longitude and degrees; and other such boring marine biology matters as the *littoral,* and various types of marine life they collected or discovered.

In scientific terms, the expedition was a huge success, for it documented hundreds of varieties and species of fish, mollusks, crustaceans, birds, and mammals.

But, in literary terms, were it not for one little entry Steinbeck made toward the end of the expedition, it reads like a sure cure for insomnia.

The *Sea of Cortez* tied up in the fishing village of La Paz for a few days—nothing unusual about that.

The interesting thing about this entry had to do with a stir of excitement in the village noted in the log by Steinbeck.

The Fly Rod Chronicles

There's a brief entry regarding a humble pearl fisherman who had found a pearl of unusual size.

This obscure reference later became the basis, the germ, the inspiration, for his famous novella *The Pearl,* which proves to me that even technical writing can be beautiful. Funny where writers find their material, isn't it?

At the end of 2002, I sat down to assess the past year's activities and accomplishments and to put down on paper my goals and resolutions for the New Year. You know the drill. But, this time, I was serious about my goals and resolutions.

I thought again about my son's comment: *You never have any fun.*

I totaled up my days fishing for 2002: an even twenty, including the three-day coho fishing trip to the Talachulitna River in Alaska. Pathetic, when you consider the investment in rods, reels, and so forth. I swore to do better in 2003.

My motto became "2003 Will Set Me Free!"

And I truly believed it. I made it a goal to fish every month of the year, and to double my 2002 output to a new total of forty times. But I had to have a plan.

First thing, I knew I'd have to finesse this thing with SWAMBO. Not an easy task. That's when I came up with the "hour-for-hour" contract. She went for it—so far, so good.

The next step was to make a list of all the places I wanted to fish. This was not as easy as it seems. I'm not rich, so finances could easily limit my options. And Utah is quite dry, or so I believed at the time; so, how could I get a variety of fishing without becoming burned out by the same places?

A Pretty Dry State

I checked the shelves at the library, then at the bookstore, for possible reference material. I found a little guidebook called *Fishing Utah*, by Brett Prettyman. There it was: a concise guide to more than 170 places I could fly fish, together with maps, travel directions, types of flies, bait, lures, and other useful tips. Eureka!

I took out a Utah road map and, using my granddaughter's compass, inscribed a red circle around Salt Lake City, representing an approximately sixty-mile radius, roughly sixty minutes of driving.

I was amazed at the number of waters that became available to me. Not all were large waters. Sure, there was the Provo and the Weber. Even the Ogden River, if you stretched a little. Most were tiny blue lines on the maps—small streams. Then there were the small blue spots—small- to medium-sized lakes and reservoirs. But they were all reported by Mr. Prettyman to be fishable; most of them year-round.

I was further amazed to see the variety of fishable *species* reported to be in those waters: perch, channel catfish, bluegill; large and small mouth bass; and their cousin, the white bass; trout in all their varieties; walleyes, pike, and muskies; even the lowly, but feisty, carp.

I won't give a detailed chronology here; that would be boring. But it is useful to point out some observations made along the way in my simple discovery, some of which are universal, and many of which have specific application to my own experience.

First—and this may be a somewhat obvious point—

The Fly Rod Chronicles

fishing close to home is kind of like the mistaken belief we had when we were teenagers, that the hometown girls weren't quite as pretty as the ones in the next town over—that's not necessarily so. Moral: I found a lot of good fishing right in my own backyard. Much of it is in surprisingly pretty spots.

Example: One summer morning I checked my list and decided it was time to visit Hobble Creek, in Utah County, just a couple miles east of the town of Springville, which, by the way, is a pretty little community on its own merits.

Hobble Creek is probably more famously known by Utah residents for its golf course and surrounding big, suburban estates. What many don't know is the good fishing to be found there. In about one hour after leaving home I was parked alongside the stream, rigged up with my seven and a half foot, four-weight, small stream rod, and casting one of Steve Beck's expertly tied, size 18 Parachute Adams. I was all alone, I mean *all alone*.

I counted myself one of the luckiest guys ever because I was alone on this pretty spot doing what I loved; no other fisherman shared the stream with me.

Second, I learned small streams do not necessarily mean small fish. Again, Hobble Creek. In one hour of fishing, I caught and released two browns over ten inches, two over thirteen inches; and broke off a lunker that looked to be about sixteen, possibly seventeen, inches that, by darn, made my hands shake after I struck him too hard. And all this on a clear little spring creek that appears to be under-fished.

Third, I found out close means cheaper. Cheaper for gas,

A Pretty Dry State

and if you count your own time as money, a lot less time spent in travel. You get there faster, and you're there doing what you went for sooner: fishing. Again, Hobble Creek. I can be there fishing in just one hour from my home. I can go up Big Cottonwood and be fishing for feisty browns and rainbows within twenty minutes. And you don't have to pay for motels and meals (unless for your own sneaky reasons you'd prefer to).

And there's another thing that factors into my way of thinking. Call it the "support-your-local-merchant syndrome." Call me old-fashioned, but I sort of have this thing about supporting most things local. You know the old saying about a prophet without honor? Well, as a contrarian, I find a lot of good reasons to stick close to home for my fishing.

Don't get me wrong; I enjoy the exotic fishing trips as much as the next guy (we'll talk about those in other chapters). I get a sense of satisfaction knowing I bought my gas from the small businessman in Duchesne, even if it cost a few pennies more a gallon. Or if I stop off to have a great breakfast at the Kamas Kafe (you know it's good if the name starts with a K or ends with an E), even though I'd rather be on the Upper Provo an hour sooner. There's something really satisfying about sitting down to an early morning meal with all the local guys and their John Deere ball caps, their coffee, and their hot, home made biscuits with sausage gravy (it's some of this country's finest, believe me).

There are a lot of small towns within a short driving distance from my home that depend on tourists and deer

The Fly Rod Chronicles

hunters and fly fishermen for their economic existence. Dutch John, and Wanship, Utah; Mac's Inn, Idaho; Dillon and Ennis, Montana, and the town of West Yellowstone easily come to mind.

I also think it's kind of cool to drop into the local hardware store in these small towns and see the displays of rods, leaders, Eagle Claw snelled hooks (still in the same familiar packaging!), and trout flies—just like when I was a kid. The flies are mostly the basic, generic patterns and sizes.

My wife's cousin runs just such a place in Swan Lake, Idaho, just ten miles south of Downey. Swan Lake was the birthplace of my wife's father. Drop into the Thomas Merc sometime and buy a Coke and chat with the owner, Kim Thomas, a third generation proprietor. He can give you some good information about local fishing spots; he's a fisherman, too. I know. I've fished with him a couple times.

I love Thomas Merc. It's not Wal-Mart; not well lighted or laid out in any organized way. The floors are made of old wood planks impregnated with oil and dirt ground in by many decades of feet. You can find just about anything needed for country living: pots, iron skillets, and Dutch ovens; bolts of fabric, patterns, needles, and thread; bag balm and various salves and ointments; Ajax cleanser, Bayer aspirins and Colgate toothpaste; even shovels and twine; and, always, a good assortment of penny candy and licorice. In the back is the post office. Nobody in Swan Lake, Idaho, has any street address; you just send letters to Swan Lake, Idaho, plus the Zip code.

A Pretty Dry State

Thomas Merc has an interesting history. Ask Kim about that, too.

But, back to the trout flies. Usually I find there are fly patterns unique to the local water, and tied, no doubt, by that weird guy who moved to that area a few years previously to get away from the Rat Race in San Francisco, who never does any *work*. He's into fly fishing in a real serious way. (Local rumor has it he made millions in some dot-com deal just before the Bubble burst.) You can buy his pretty flies for seventy-five cents apiece. They're pretty good, well-tied flies. Obviously, he's not into fly tying for the money.

These spots are also a good source of local info on what the fish are biting (reference Kim Thomas, above). I'm also very fond of the Dam Store in Swan Valley, Idaho (not to be confused with Swan Lake). It's very close to the boat basin, just below the Palisades Dam on the South Fork. It's a lot like Thomas Merc. Its motto: "Best store by a dam site." I love that.

Then there's Bob's Qwik Stop, just off Highway 20 in Rigby, Idaho, on the way to West Yellowstone. (Actually, there are quite a few establishments in and around Rigby named Bob's this or Bob's that.) Stop in for gas and try some of their local, hand dipped ice cream cones. And take a minute to look at the many mounted trophy fish that decorate the walls. When you do, I'll bet you'll wish you could talk to the guys that caught them and learn what they were using. Those neat-looking flies in the glass case will be tied by—you guessed it—Steve Beck.

The Fly Rod Chronicles

Just across the road is the South Fork Inn, a nice, clean, inexpensive motel that caters to fly fishermen, too. It's only about four or five miles up the road to the South Fork. And you can buy your license right close by at Bob's.

Please don't ever sell these small town people short. It's because they depend somewhat on our money (meaning that of deer hunters, fly fishermen and tourists), that they're likely to spend some time learning about our sport and how to be of service to our needs.

I'm never really surprised to see some of the local boys, farmer tans, John Deere caps and all, out there throwing nymphs or dry flies with some pretty basic fly rods, reels and other gear; catching and releasing trout, cheek-to-cheek with the best of the city dudes and their fancy catalog outfits. In fact, I get a secret pleasure when I see Willard, the local guy, outcast and out-fish Kevin, the city guy.

Probably just as much pleasure as Willard gets.

Chapter 11

Combat Pay

It was early January 1971. My friend, Lieutenant (junior grade) Mike Sessions, and I were on board an Air Force tanker jet flying west from Guam to Bangkok, Thailand. We were both in the Navy at the time. I was just a few days away from completing my tour of duty with the Reserves. We had wangled a couple days of "basket" leave: a pass given by our commanding officers allowing us to take a couple days off without deducting from our official leave.

The Fly Rod Chronicles

We managed to hook up with a jet and crew, a midnight flight from Andersen AFB. The crew from Ellsworth AFB in South Dakota had stopped in Guam to refuel, before continuing on to an airbase near Bangkok, for six months of TDY (temporary duty).

We fell asleep shortly after takeoff. I slept for several hours and, just before dawn, I was wakened by the sensation that we were turning sharply. I looked out a porthole and saw city lights 35,000 feet below. I asked one of the crew what was happening.

"That's Saigon down there. We're making a detour in over the war zone…for *combat pay*. Then we'll go back out over the Gulf of Siam, on up to Utapao."

He winked as if I knew what he meant.

"Combat pay?"

"Yeah, you know, we get two months tax-free combat pay just by flying *over* the zone."

Cool, I thought. Maybe I could apply for some. I never did; too much paperwork.

#

A couple of years ago, when Mark and I were in Alaska fly fishing for salmon, I thought of that night many years ago.

My brother-in-law, Doug Dickey, loaned us his pickup so I could drive Mark from Anchorage down the Kenai Peninsula to Seward, and perhaps stop to try for rainbows and Bull Trout in one of the many streams on the way.

Combat Pay

I made a specific point of slowing down as we approached the Kenai River so Mark could see firsthand the hundreds of fishermen standing literally shoulder-to-shoulder, casting for salmon along the riverbanks. In Alaska they call it "combat fishing." I've seen it elsewhere on other waters when there's a special run of something going on.

These guys are there with "gear" (spinning or bait casting outfits, with heavy duty line, big chunks of lead weight and large, multiple hooks). These guys are serious meat hunters. I have personally witnessed fishermen on the Kenai hook a fish, horse it in, make two filets, drop the filets into a plastic bag, and fling the still-twitching carcass (mouth opening and closing, eyes wildly blinking, gasping for oxygen) back into the river, set up the rig, cast, and continue on fishing, all in the space of a couple of minutes of elapsed time. They dream up a lot of wacky contests in Alaska to pass the time. It's possible they even have some sort of Kenai Sockeye Catch-Clean-Bait Up-Recast Tournament. I don't know.

Stream etiquette is non-existent in this harvest atmosphere. You catch a fish and step out of the line, the line closes up to take your place. You have to actually *elbow* your way back into line. I have witnessed fist fights break out in this highly charged crowd. Reminds me of outdoor films I've seen of bears fighting during the salmon run.

I had come close to erupting myself just a few days earlier on the Talchulitna River. The second day we were there, a group of firemen from Upstate New York arrived. They immediately marked themselves as clods, breaking the wonderful quiet with their loud laughter, drinking on the river, and swearing; and, worst of all, flinging their "gear" over the tops of our lines.

I reached my limit when one of them cast over me while I was playing an especially frisky silver. Luckily, I didn't lose the fish, though I did lose my cool and swore at the guy—something I hardly ever do.

I think I recall yelling something like, "If I'd wanted (expletive) combat fishing, I would'a gone combat fishing on the (expletive) Kenai!"

I only got a lot of loud laughs from that bunch; they thought I was trying to be funny.

#

Then, there was the time recently on the Provo, a perfect fall evening on one of my last trips that season. I came upon one of my favorite spots just before sundown; I had been saving it for the "last cast," if you know what I mean. I had been pretty lucky to be there that evening; there was a prolific caddis hatch of at least three different kinds and I had caught several nice fish. I don't remember how many, which is partly the point here.

Then I witnessed one of those rare moments on a trout stream. The sky was suddenly filled with mayfly spinners that sparkled like flashes of fire in the slanting rays of sunshine. Fish were jumping everywhere, but I was so dazzled by this sight, I forgot to change flies and start casting.

Combat Pay

And, suddenly, it was over.

The sun slipped behind Mount Timpanogos; the air began to cool, so I moved on.

I came around the bend of the stream, hoping nobody else would be there in the spot I was saving for last. There was. Another fisherman was at the tail of the pool, a long, gently bending run that flows below a nice gravel bar and riffle, then tails over another gravel bar, divides and makes a double riffle.

As you're supposed to, I asked him if he minded if I fished the riffle up above. He said no problem, there's plenty of room, etc. So I made a wide detour out around him and approached my spot well above him, probably thirty-five or forty yards away at least.

I knew I had one last shot, so I debated between a Blue Winged Olive or a Pale Morning Dun. I chose a #20 BWO (the last one left in my fly box). I sharpened the hook, tied it on to a 6x tippet and greased it up. I made one of those rare lucky casts: I false cast a couple times and floated the little fly out over the lip of the gravel bar face, watching the fly settle gently down onto the foam, at the seam where the stream defines itself again into riffle water.

About two seconds after the fly touched down, the water erupted into spray. I struck gently and the trout was on. I could tell by the heft of the fish and the power of its struggle against the line that this was a nice one. He would be the perfect end to my perfect evening and to a near-perfect season of fly fishing.

The Fly Rod Chronicles

I got him on the reel and tried to keep it in the shallower riffle water closest to me. The fish had other ideas; he turned and began his run downstream, racing for the deeper, stronger currents and the tail of the pool, taking line off the reel as he went. I was almost into my backing when I remembered to call out to the other guy, "Fish on!" He grudgingly reeled in, taking his own sweet time to give me the room I would need.

He immediately began coaching me with directions like: "Keep your rod tip up!" "Don't horse him, he looks pretty big!" "Keep him away from those snags over there!" etc. Like, I need advice? I *think* I know what I'm doing here!

The fish began to tire. I had two choices for landing him: one side—Loudmouthed Fisherman's side—was still, shallow water. The other side was the gravel bar at the pool's shallow end, actually closer to where I was playing the trout.

I confess, I was now so annoyed by the guy I figured I'd rub my success in his face—just a little. I let the big brown fin his way slowly toward the other bank, Loudmouth's side, and I followed, slowly, very slowly. Finally, I was right in front of this other guy and I got a good look at him and his gear: yep, high-end Sage rod, Simms best waders, Patagonia's best vest, etc., etc. Fancy catalog stuff.

I started to palm the fish, which is better for the trout, and the trouble started. Mr. Expert sticks his net in my face.

"I always think it's really better if you *net* them."

Really? Says who?

But I kept my cool, accepted his net, and started to make my move.

Combat Pay

"Head first is best, I always say."

Oh, shut up!

"Want to take a picture? Do you have a camera?"

I was glad I did; I certainly did *not* want to be indebted to this idiot; nor did I want to later have to beg a copy. Then he'd want to be pen pals for sure. At the risk of being criticized for doing it with the wrong hand, I pulled my camera out and handed it to him.

"Better hurry; only time for one shot. I always like to get them back into the water as fast as possible."

This "hurry" instruction from the guy taking the picture!

I gritted my teeth and tried to smile; you can see my cheesiest grin ever in this picture. Is that because I'm clamping down on some choice obscenities?

"Thanks," was all I dared say, as I released this fat, butter-yellow twenty-inch brown with the prettiest spotting I had ever seen. It was almost ready to spawn; I guessed it to be close to five pounds. Okay, maybe he was only four, but if Mr. Expert had asked, I would have said, "SIX POUNDS AT LEAST!"

Now, whenever I look at that picture, I try hard to remember the beautiful fall evening; that spectacular spinner fall; the way that brown shot up out of the water after that fly; the adrenaline rush as I played him to my hand.

I try *not* to remember that obnoxious jerk. I'm sure he meant well, but I can't help thinking: here's a guy I do *not* want as my fishing buddy. Ever. For many reasons. One good reason: no combat pay.

The Fly Rod Chronicles

###

Contrast that experience with this: Several years ago I was in Tokyo with a client, staying at a posh hotel. One morning as I got on the elevator to go down to breakfast, a hand stuck through and held back the closing door. In stepped a smartly dressed Japanese businessman. In one hand he lugged a bulging leather briefcase. In the other hand, he toted a metal tube.

It looked a lot like a fly rod case to me. I was curious; I had heard there were a lot of Japanese who loved fly fishing. The Japanese are great joiners; they belong to a lot of clubs and societies. Supposedly, there are more than ten thousand fly-fishing clubs in Japan.

I spoke a greeting to him in Japanese. Then I spoke English. "I'm curious. Either you're an architect, or that's a fly rod under your arm."

He grinned and replied in perfect English, "Some plans for our business. I wish it was my fly rod."

"You're a fly fisherman, then?"

"Yes, when I have the time."

The elevator hit the lobby floor and we got off. We chatted for a while and traded business cards. We promised to correspond by e-mail. I promised to get together some day; he would be my guest to fish the Provo River. He said he'd heard a lot about it, but never had the good fortune to fish in the West.

Combat Pay

About a year later I got an e-mail from Mark (actually Makito Oishi, but, like many Japanese, he has an American nickname), saying he would soon be in Los Angeles for some company meetings. He works for the Puma sportswear and equipment people.

We made arrangements for him to come to Salt Lake and fish the Provo with me. I wanted to do it right, so I arranged for a guide from one of our local fly shops.

We spent a couple of great days in early July, mostly fishing nymphs, but occasionally throwing some caddis flies. Mark, it turns out, had fished some really great trout, salmon, and steelhead waters: Norway, England, Scotland, Ireland, Spain, Germany, France. I even think he mentioned Czech Republic. Or was it Bosnia or Yugoslavia?

This guy was no beginner; he had some great equipment, not necessarily expensive, but good quality stuff. And there was no doubt he knew how to use it. He caught two trout for every one of mine. He was not a scorekeeper; not once did he mention how many fish he caught, or how many I had caught. He was a gracious guest and a lot of fun to fish with.

And that's the point: It's as important with *whom* you fish as where and for what you fish. I've had some great times fishing; I've been very lucky to get in on some good trips to some legendary waters because I was at the right place at the right time.

But I think the greater fortune has been the luck of *who* I got to fish with.

I'm also remembering an early Saturday morning in the

The Fly Rod Chronicles

spring of 1978. The doorbell rang; I answered in my pajamas. On the doorstep stood Ben, his arms loaded with what looked like fishing gear. I thought he had come to invite me fishing; I dimly recalled talking about our going fishing together some day.

"These are for you," he said, pushing the load of stuff at me.

"What for?" I asked.

"We're even now. Now I pay you. We're even."

He turned around and walked to his battered pickup. I never talked to Ben again.

Ben worked as a body and fender man; he had a major drinking problem. When he wasn't working, he was fishing or tying flies. He was very good at both, judging from the pictures he showed me and the mess of fat rainbows he brought me from one trip to the Wind River Reservation in Wyoming.

Ben's drinking problem got him a long string of DUI charges, which he ignored. Finally one day he was arrested. He called me, and I got him out. I met with several different prosecutors and judges and got his charges reduced. He still lost his driving privileges. That didn't seem to stop him.

Ben never had any cash to pay me my fees, but then that day he showed up on my doorstep with the fishing gear: a pair of chest waders, a new Fenwick HMG graphite rod (an eight-and-a-half foot, five-weight), a Pflueger Medalist (I love to joke with my fishing partners by pronouncing the *P*) single-action fly reel loaded with new line, and a fly box full of nymphs and streamers Ben had tied himself. Now what?

Combat Pay

Those many years ago, my neighbor and friend, Mike Bennett, took the time and trouble to teach me how to fly fish. Step One: How to cast a fly line. Until then, nobody had helped me and I hadn't asked. Mike had learned from his dad, Lefty, a high school history teacher. I don't know who taught Lefty. Others have taught and helped me over the years, including my son, Mark and a few of his friends. And, I've been lucky to fish with a lot of good fishermen and guides who have taught me well.

So what *does* make a good fishing companion? What makes a bad one?

Here's my opinion of what makes a *good* one:
- Does not bring a dog along, especially in a boat (unless said dog is trained in fly fishing and boat etiquette, like Mark's chocolate lab, Steve).
- Does not coach techniques while you're fishing (except when asked).
- Does not borrow rods, flies, money, truck, etc., except in a dire emergency.
- Does not brag (especially about size/number of fish, equipment cost/brands, income, killing made in stock market/401K, drinking capacity, number of ex-wives, or sexual exploits).
- Does not offer opinions. Exception: freely/honestly, when asked.
- Does offer to split costs of trip, and then performs.
- Does offer to drive vehicle on long trips.
- Does bring/pay for his share of gas, food, drink, motel,

etc.
- Offers to bring his boat (if he has one) without being asked.
- Does not keep a running count of who caught how many fish and what size. (Exception: if friendly bets are in play.)

I'm sure I could think of many more, but you get the point. Have some fun and make your own list here.

#

The thing I'm after when I'm fishing, even more than the fish, is *solitude*. I want, I *need*, to get away from the battle zone of life from time to time. Everyone has the same need to a greater or lesser degree. Solitude is a rare commodity these days, hard to come by. The sweet solitude I need and enjoy on the river can either be enhanced by a fishing buddy who understands and has the same needs, or it can be ruined by the wrong choice of a fishing companion. (I think here of the words of Ernest Schwiebert: "Many rivers have become a carnival of bad manners.")

Fly fishing, unlike other sports, is *not* combat, so why make it that way? Especially when you're not drawing combat pay.

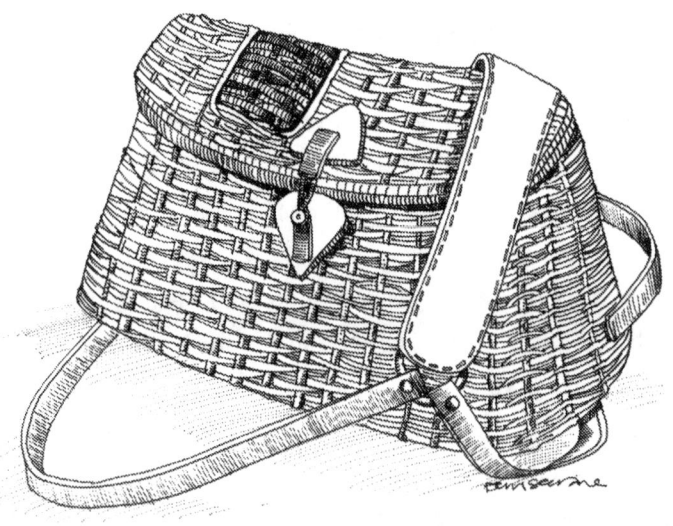

CHAPTER 12

Old Spice

Have you ever been in a business meeting, in an elevator, or in any other close quarters and been assaulted by the overwhelming odor of some other guy's cologne?

Dress for Success tip: Never splash on any of the strong stuff before a business meeting. If anything, use some Deep Woods. That'll prove you're an outdoorsman.

I remember one time when I was golfing and we could smell some guy's cologne upwind from us. We were on the fairway

The Fly Rod Chronicles

at Willow Creek, on the approach to the green. Someone in the foursome ahead of us, on the green about seventy yards away, had on some pretty strong stuff. I wondered how his golfing partners could stand it.

The guys I golf with would have ragged his butt without mercy from the first tee.

Men's fragrances just aren't the same as they used to be. When I was younger, the men in my life—my Dad, uncles, neighbors, guys at church, bosses, high school teachers and coaches—all wore straightforward, simple stuff: Aqua Velva, Mennen, Old Spice, Bay Rum. That was pretty much it, unless you were adventurous and splashed on some Yardley's English Lavender. I knew one old peach farmer in Yuba City who used nothing but Jergens Lotion. He had a skin problem, but, also, he just liked the smell of it.

The choices for fly rods in those days were rather narrow, too: It was either bamboo or fiber glass. You could have your glass rod in a solid material or a hollow construction. There weren't more than a couple dozen brands, and a lot of those were "production" rods sold through retail mass marketers such as Sears, Montgomery Ward, and various hardware store chains. That was during the '50s and '60s.

Then came the late '60s and into the '70s. Bamboo as a rod-building material faded out in favor of glass, then, even glass was fast giving way to the newer space age material: graphite. And Old Spice, Mennen and Aqua Velva? They were fast being joined and pushed aside by some new fragrances with neater packaging and more exotic names: Canoe, English

Old Spice

Leather, Jade, and Elsha, for example.

Today I see a weird correlation between the proliferation of men's fragrances and the boutique marketing of fly rods. Now there are probably a hundred different men's fragrances on the market, perhaps more. I'm sure there are at least that many brands of fly rods available.

Each new year I observe rapid advances in the science and technology of fly-rod materials, as chronicled in the catalogs I get from Orvis, L.L. Bean, Thomas & Thomas, Redington, St. Croix, Sage, Scott, Winston, Loomis, and Cabela's. The same goes with the companion equipment: reels, lines, leader materials. There's a flood of float tubes, waders, wading shoes, jackets, and other clothing. Kick boat companies and float boat companies are springing up like mushrooms after a rainstorm. And that's just the hardware-type stuff associated with fly fishing.

What about the vast catalog of other gear: flies, lures, floatant dope, fly-tying outfits, hook retractors, fly boxes and wallets, as a small sampling.

When I first started getting serious about fishing with a fly rod in the early '50s in a small community in Northern California called Bald Rock, my friend, Ron Salisbury, and I fished with the following basic equipment: three-piece, eight-and-a-half or nine-foot split bamboo fly rods with extra tips (his was a spiffy new Montague; at that time, mine was the nameless Japanese metal telescoping model I'd found in the garage); a single action reel, level fly line, snelled bait hooks, split shot, a few flies, a good pocket knife, a spool of leader

The Fly Rod Chronicles

material, and a bait can (Hills Bros. Coffee, red, one pound). We also had split willow, leather-bound creels (baskets) to carry the fish we caught. We'd nestle them in sweet ferns to keep them fresh. Except for the Hills Bros. Coffee can, we could carry all of our fishing gear in our jeans pockets or the one leather pocket stitched to the front of our creel.

Almost every summer day after morning chores were done, Ron and I spent our free time fishing the many small creeks close to home—Berry Creek, Brush Creek, and several little nameless spring creeks that ran through cow pastures—for native rainbows and browns. We also fished Lake Madrone for channel cats and bluegills when trout fishing was slow. The bluegills were always eager and willing and the catfish made good eating.

Back then we were too young to shave, but we had some opinions already forming about our favorite after shave. Ron's was Aqua Velva; mine was Old Spice. We also had some definite opinions about our favorite soft drink. He favored Pepsi; I tended toward the citrus drinks, like 7-Up or Squirt. (Ron tends toward Jim Beam, now. Me? I'm a Gelusil guy!)

We didn't even know what waders were. We fished in blue jeans and tennis shoes. We didn't have a car, we weren't old enough to drive anyway, so we walked a few miles to and from the creeks each day. We carried sandwiches wrapped in waxed paper and aluminum foil in our creels, along with a bottle of pop to cool in the creek. For a nickel we could buy a bag of Planters peanuts or a Snickers bar at the country store.

Life was simple; life was sweet. We always caught a

Old Spice

few fish, some days a lot. Sometimes we even caught a few monsters over twelve inches. Sometimes our moms let us camp overnight down in the bottom of Bald Rock Canyon so we could fish the Middle Fork of the mighty Feather River. We took only our fishing stuff, some matches, and a can each of stew or chili for our supper; and that was sometimes supplemented by a few big browns we caught and roasted over live coals.

It was a long, steep hike back out of that hole, even for young guys. Our fishing rods were the only things we took back out. We buried the tin cans, along with a couple of pans and some utensils for the next time down. I think they might be there still.

I look back on those sweet younger days and wish in some ways I could return to the simpler approach to fishing we had then. We lived the Huck Finn existence. We didn't need a lot of stuff, nor could we afford it. Any spare money went for school clothes or shotgun shells, not for upgrading the old fly rod or reel. What we had got the job done.

As I look back, I also remember certain smells. It seems our sense of smell is important to our learning process and aromas and certain fragrances can trigger memories from way back in our past. For example, whenever any one says the word, "skunk," or I get a whiff of skunk scent, I have an instant memory.

Again, it was while we were living in Bald Rock. Since there was a chronic shortage of cash for spending money, we were constantly on the prowl for money-making projects.

The Fly Rod Chronicles

We cut firewood, we split cedar logs for fence posts, and we picked raspberries and strawberries for a local farmer. We collected and sold fresh Christmas trees and pinecones, holly, mistletoe and fir boughs during the holiday season. I even gathered dogwood berries and maple seeds to sell to a nursery in Oroville.

There were a lot of wild animals around our place; so, in the winter, I also ran a trap line. I caught foxes, raccoons, and mink, selling their pelts for cash. That's why I caught and froze a large supply of bluegills each summer: for trap bait.

One disadvantage to the trapping business was skunks. For every good fur-bearing animal, I'd catch at least two skunks; what to do with them was always a problem. Then my older brother, Norman, came up with a brilliant plan.

Norman had read an article in *The Reader's Digest* about how perfume was made. One major ingredient, he said, was skunk oil, and he added that the stuff was worth hundreds of dollars per ounce—liquid gold!

"That's what makes their scent," I said.

Exactly.

Although we lived on a small farm and had seen or helped in the slaughter of a lot of animals—such as chickens, hogs, cattle, and also a few wild ones such as deer, pheasant, quail, squirrels—we didn't have a clue about skunk anatomy. We should have done more research.

We didn't have to wait long for our first skunk oil harvest. The next morning I had a skunk in one of my traps. I dragged it home and nailed it up on the big cedar tree in the yard just

Old Spice

outside the house where I always did my pelt skinning.

"What now?" I asked Norman.

He sharpened his hunting knife razor-sharp, found a Mason quart jar, and then handed me the knife.

"I'll hold the jar," he said. "You cut."

What happened next is still kind of a blur in my memory. The best I can recall, I made a deep cut just below the poor critter's bumhole (which made some sense, because I had witnessed a few skunks raise their tails just before they sprayed our dog, Frio), while Norman held the jar to catch the liquid gold. We weren't prepared for the results.

Smelling skunk scent out in the open air, some distance from the skunk, where the scent is widely distributed through the air, is one thing. But smelling the highly concentrated scent up close is a different experience.

Picture this in the rapid sequence of just a few seconds: I made the cut; the dark yellow stuff gushed out; Norman dropped the jar, we both stumbled back, vomiting violently, and ran for the house. A couple of our younger brothers came running outside when they heard the commotion. Then they ran back into the house, vomiting violently. What a mess!

We huddled to see what our next move should be. First, we didn't want our parents to come home and see what a stupid thing we had done. Second, and more immediate, we needed to remove the offending carcass from the tree and get it far, far away from the house. Naturally, I was elected.

You've heard of the ten-foot pole? I found one even longer, attached a piece of wire coat hanger to the end and

The Fly Rod Chronicles

snagged the skunk from the skinning tree. I must have looked pretty silly carrying that pole over my shoulder like I was headed to the old fishing hole, which was sort of my plan.

Down in the pasture, about a quarter mile from the house, ran a pretty little spring-fed creek. It had a few minnows and chubs, but no trout. I headed for the creek, determined to dunk the skunk, hoping to wash away the scent. I plunked it into the deepest pool, thinking it would sink to the bottom. I had forgotten that animals float. I watched in horror as it bobbed to the surface, floating in its own rainbow-colored oil slick!

The folks came home a few hours later.

"Where's the skunk?" Dad yelled.

The smell around there lasted for a couple days. But the memory will last forever.

#

Many years later, when I was in Seward, Alaska, I thought of that awful skunk oil slick, polluting that sparkling little creek. Janet and I were there on vacation. We visited the Marine Life Study Center, established mostly by settlement trust funds paid by the Exxon oil company after the *Valdez* oil tanker disaster. It houses many species of marine life: penguins, puffins, ducks and other birds. There are sea lions and seals, and walruses, too. But no Orcas. Marine biologists and scientists come from all over the world to study and research there.

The most interesting part for me was the basement section,

Old Spice

which held over a dozen huge tanks of salmon in sea water. The water was pumped in from the adjacent Resurrection Bay; it circulated constantly and was temperature controlled. Each big tank held hundreds of salmon in ascending ages, from literally small fry, to adult spawners.

I asked one of the guides on duty a few questions about the salmon. I was amazed that one experiment they were conducting was the release of adult fish into the ocean, tagged with special high-tech, electronic tracking devices. These fish were hatched from eggs gathered and fertilized from *within the laboratory*! The scientists wanted to see if the fish would return to this site when it came time for them to spawn.

I asked the guide how they find their way back. Is there any working scientific theory about migration? He said they were working on one new theory: That salmon find their way back to the waters where they were spawned by *smell*. That is, they use their keen olfactory nerves to literally smell and sort through who knows how many different traces of minerals or other elements dissolved in minute particles throughout the water to guide them back home. In other words, certain *smells* in the water were "in [their] memory locked," as Shakespeare said. These odoriferous *footprints* or codes, became permanently printed in their brains, stored away until the time came to call on those codes to guide them back home to fill the measure of their creation.

So there you have it. Back to the smells of early childhood. Think of the smells that trigger pleasant experiences or memories from your past. Think about fresh raspberries, or alfalfa hay, or licorice, or popcorn. What do you recall? Or what if you say Chanel No. 5? Or what about a sea breeze? I think fondly of crushed ferns. I can still conjure up the pleasant, warm smell of milk fresh from Millie, our cow. And when I do, I remember a gaggle of nameless barn kittens that waited nearby for the moment when I'd playfully squirt a teat-full at them to wet their faces.

Simple smells, simple memories, simple times.

And that brings me back to *stuff*.

How many rods does a guy need, for example? And what brand name or price tag do they have to carry?

Okay, so here's my ideal arsenal of rods: One six-and-a-half- or seven-foot, three- or four-weight, for small streams or pan fish. One eight-foot, five-weight, for larger streams like the Provo and for throwing dries and nymphs. One eight-and-a-half-foot, six- or seven-weight for bigger nymphs, dries, and streamers on big streams and some of the big rivers like the South Fork or the Green. And one nine- or nine-and-a-half-foot, eight- or nine-weight, for steelhead, stripers, big bass, salmon, or float tubing on lakes or big ponds I can't wade.. And, of course, reels and lines to match.

I may have said this before, but I have a bias in favor of bamboo rods, mostly because I like the feel of them and the way they match my slower casting stroke. But I suppose I'm a little guilty of being nostalgic, too.

The rest of the stuff is purely personal, but I like a casting shirt with big pockets and one fly box with a wide selection of flies that I choose in advance for the outing; no need then

Old Spice

to wear a vest.

I prefer Gore-Tex to neoprene waders (in winter I wear insulated long johns, less interior "sweating"); and I favor the guide-pants style over the chest-type waders. In hot weather I'll often just wear wading shoes or even sandals and shorts and wade "wet."

And, of course, there are the gadgets: gink, forceps, nippers, spools of leader and tippet material. I carry that stuff on a lanyard around my neck.

Two last items: magnifying reading glasses and the indispensable polarized glasses, for protection from both the sun and wind-thrown hooks.

There. You have one man's simple approach to fly fishing...

And I still favor Old Spice.

The Fly Rod Chronicles

CHAPTER 13

Restoring The Rapidan

A couple of summers ago, I was cleaning out the garage. It's an annual affair, a hot, dusty job. I have to wear one of those painter's masks; there's serious danger of Hantavirus from the field mice that winter there.

I came across an orange-colored cardboard tube with a rusted metal screw cap. At first, I thought it contained some of Janet's old watercolors or some posters for her classroom bulletin boards. I shook it—a definite rattling sound, not the

The Fly Rod Chronicles

sound paper makes. *Could it be an old fiberglass spinning rod?* I wondered. The cap was stuck so tightly that it took WD-40 and pair of channel-lock pliers to loosen it.

I tipped the tube and out slid an old bamboo fly rod. It was my old Montague Rapidan! My first real fly rod.

A wave of emotions swept over me: sadness, then guilt. Sadness because it was in pretty bad shape: several guides were missing, others were loose, and the silk windings were frayed and brittle. The cork grip looked like field mice had made a meal of it; the bakelite reel seat was cracked, the butt cap missing. Both tip sections had bad "sets" to them; one was missing the tip top guide. How and when did I let it get into such bad shape? When did I put it on the shelf? Was it about the same time I got the new Fenwick graphite rod from Ben in 1978?

Then I felt a little guilt because this rod had been a good friend to me for so many years, until I changed over to that Fenwick graphite. Hey, times change; you have to move with the times, don't you? But this was the treatment I gave the Rapidan in return?

It was dust-covered. I got out a car-washing towel. As I wiped off the accumulated grime, I began to wonder if the Rapidan's days were over. Or was it possible to give it a second life? I carefully jointed it up; the ferrule between the butt and mid-section was a little loose. I rubbed the male ferrule alongside my nose and it made a tighter fit.

My memory flashed back about forty-five years or so, remembering how my friend, Don Turnbaugh, taught me that

Restoring The Rapidan

trick of rubbing the ferrule against my nose when the Rapidan was shiny and brand new. I remembered how I'd put a really deep set in one tip fighting a twenty-pound carp caught on a night crawler one early spring Saturday (now I read about carp being a game fish).

I wondered if it was possible to restore it, as I waggled it out in the driveway. It still felt very much alive. The dark honey color of the bamboo wood still gleamed in the sunlight, but there were several spots where the spar varnish had rubbed away or scratched off. It still bore the Montague original decal on the butt section; I wondered what had happened to the cloth sock and original tube.

I located a spare sock in my fishing closet, slid the rod back into the cardboard tube, placed it in my fly-fishing closet, where it was to stay for another year.

All the next year I'd see that orange tube each time I opened the closet. Memories would fill my thoughts, and I'd be caught up in pleasant recollections for days.

Times when, as a kid, I would fish Berry Creek and Brush Creek and the Middle Fork of the Feather River, usually with Ron Salisbury or Don Turnbaugh. Times when we dug night crawlers or red wiggler worms. Or when we chased fat black crickets or grasshoppers for bait. I remembered the tiny red and white Daredevil spinners we tied on and lobbed up and across the currents, letting them drift down below, then slowly hand retrieving line, then the tug, the hook set, then the fight. Sometimes it was a small, single-bladed brass or copper spinner with a single, size 12 treble hook. Same results

The Fly Rod Chronicles

as when I throw big streamers now.

I remembered the many wild rainbows and browns we caught, killed, and ate, sometimes for dinner as we camped on a sandbar. Huck and Tom we were. I thought of the many fat bluegills in Lake Madrone, when the heat made the trout sulk and the cheery little bluegills let us learn and practice our primitive, self-taught fly-casting skills (the lob, later the roll cast). I remembered how sometimes as many as a half dozen bluegills would come rushing up from the green depths at my Silver Doctor, Royal Coachman, or one of my own badly-tied bumblebee patterns. Man, did they love bright colors!

I smelled crushed ferns. I smelled the marshy black mud laced with cow pats at Zink's farm, when we would sink up to our ankles in the meadows. The best fishing was on old man Zink's place: a spring-creek section that fed into Berry Creek, with long, flat pools, shaded by overhanging alder and bay laurel trees. I remember the spicy-sweet smell of crushed laurel leaves that we rubbed on our hands to cover the fishy smell.

I pictured in my mind fat browns finning lazily on the white, sandy bottom of that spring creek, lying in narrow lanes between clumps of green weeds. Sunny days and mineral-rich water produced an abundance of aquatic food. Watercress grew along the banks, trailing down into the clear water. At the end of the day I would take home a creel-full of the spicy, aromatic herb for my Dad who loved it in salads or sandwiches.

I thought how this stretch of water was like so many other

Restoring The Rapidan

spring creeks I had learned to fish over the ensuing years. On Berry Creek, you had to crawl the last ten or fifteen yards on your belly through the spongy pasture, carefully picking your way through the many cow pats. A shadow, a waving rod, a sloppy cast, and the skittish browns would shoot away to hide under the green weeds or the cut banks, leaving trails of sandy little cyclones sparkling with flecks of mica.

But if you were careful, or lucky, and could crawl behind a clump of stubby willows where the cows had grazed the bark off the trunks, you could approach closer. Keeping the sun behind you and swinging a live cricket a couple feet ahead of the trout, letting it land softly on the water with no splashing effect, then maybe...

As I remembered our boyish efforts, it dawned on me they were almost the same methods I would later learn to use with artificial flies: same approach, same presentation tactics as taught by Joe Brooks, Lefty Kreh, Jack Dennis, Leon Chandler, et al. No different, really, than when we would *present* those live night crawlers and bugs many years ago. You had to gently flip the night crawler, cricket or small hopper so it wouldn't splash down. If you cast too hard, you could flip the soft bug off the hook into the bushes.

When I first started fishing Berry Creek, the only casting I knew was what we called the "flip" or a roll cast. Then there was the "arrow" for the smaller, brushy feeder creeks, where you pulled a small amount of line very taut, bent your rod almost double like a bow, aimed, and let the bait fly at your target area. This was almost always necessary because of the low overhanging brushy conditions. You had to get the bait or lure back under the brush, into the shadows where the trout hung out.

Another variation of our casting techniques was the one we used on the bigger waters of the Feather River, where we used small Daredevil spinners or the smallest size froggy-looking Flatfish. You'd strip out about as much line as you thought would reach the target area, letting it fall loosely at your feet (this was decades before such fancy stuff as stripping baskets). Then you'd wind the rod around in a sort of slingshot arc and let the line go. If you were lucky, it would hit the target area; you then stripped line back in with a strike or, otherwise, you started all over again. Recently, watching a show demonstrating spey casting, it looked almost the same to me.

So I had never really done what you'd call *pure* fly casting with the Rapidan. I wanted to badly now, and I guess that's what prompted me to return to bamboo. I was curious to see if it was everything I'd read about during the intervening years, especially in the classic book, *Fishing Bamboo*, by John Gierach. Through reading, I became familiar with all the names of the great bamboo rod makers: Leonard; Wes Jordan; Hardy; Thomas & Thomas; R.L. Winston, Glenn;Brackett, Dickerson; A.J. Thramer; Phillipson; Pezon et Michel; Hoagy Carmichael, Jr.; Walt Garrison; plus a lot of new, younger guys like Mike Clark and Tim Zietak.

I was even surprised when I recently learned that E.C. Powell lived and had his shop in Marysville, right across the

Restoring The Rapidan

Feather River from my hometown of Yuba City. Then his son, Walton, and later his son-in-law, Tony Maslan, continued the tradition, building bamboo fly rods in Marysville. I now have a beautiful salmon-steelhead bamboo rod, the blanks of which were reputedly made in the Powell shop. Some day I'll have to travel to Marysville to have it checked out for provenance.

#

Nostalgia aside, Salt Lake City is a long way from the places you normally associate with classic bamboo fly rods: the Battenkill and Beaverkill, the Delaware, Pennsylvania chalk streams. We're a long way from the Rapidan River itself, so eloquently written about by Howell Raines in his book, *Fly Fishing Through the Midlife Crisis*.

No, Salt Lake City is out West; and out West we go for a different kind of wand: the eight-and-a-half to nine-and-a-half foot fast-action graphite, thank you. Wind conditions, big rivers and all that. Not a lot of folks out here into bamboo. Or so you might guess.

My first challenge was to get the beat-up Rapidan in shape to fish. That became obvious when I lawn cast it in the park across the street. I used several lines, finally settling on the "feel" of a six-weight double taper and a seven-weight WF. But who could fix the thing up? I certainly lacked the skills; and my sands of time were fast running low. At my age, there's a certain urgency to life.

I started asking around. Lots of dead ends. Then a kid

The Fly Rod Chronicles

at Sportsmen's Warehouse referred me to a "guy who made rods." Vague reference; no details.

The-Guy-Who-Made-Rods took over the Rapidan. I never met him, don't even remember his name. A couple weeks later, Sportsmen's called and said the rod was done. Excitedly, I drove over to pick it up. My first look at the refurb dazzled me: red and green, Christmassy-looking silks, a new tip top; the varnish gleamed in the parking lot sun. I was elated. I was eager to get up on the Provo and let the "new" 'dan do its stuff.

I hustled up to the Provo for an evening PMD hatch, strung on a line, leader, and a #18 PMD. A few false casts and I was ready.

My first presentation hit the water a little hard, I thought. A strong gust of air? Tippet too heavy? I cast again; same result: Fly splashes down hard onto water. Trout doesn't take fly. Trout disappears.

I retrieved the fly and false cast a few more times, away from the stream. Something was wrong; I could feel it, but couldn't identify *what*. Had I been using graphite for too many years now to make bamboo work? Or didn't I remember how bamboo used to work for me? What was wrong? I took the rod down and walked back to the Jeep, puzzled.

The problem gripped me for several days after. It became a BIG ISSUE. Bamboo was supposed to come alive in your hand, wasn't it? This thing didn't have a life; in fact, it was pretty dull. Stiff. Lifeless. It wasn't the lively Rapidan I remembered.

Restoring The Rapidan

I took it from the case again, examined it carefully. Then it came to me: The pictures of Orvis and other bamboo rods in the catalogs did not have very many, if any, intermediate wraps between the guides. This thing had intermediates about every two inches! That could contribute to its stiffness, couldn't it?

Then I flexed and bent each section as far as I dared and quickly released the tension: There was no *spring* to it, only stiff resistance. I examined the guide windings more closely and ran my fingers over them. They should be flat, I thought. These were bulgy. Then I saw the problem: epoxy! It looked like the whole rod had been coated in epoxy. Epoxy made it stiff, also adding to its overall weight (it did seem a lot heavier than I remembered). It felt and acted more like a Louisville Slugger than a fly rod.

I sadly put it away for a year. During that year I swatted up on my bamboo knowledge by reading; I talked to anyone who would listen. I scoured the Internet for information. I searched for someone who specialized in restoring bamboo rods. I sent the rod away to two different guys; I showed it to three local guys.

"Not interested," was the reply. "It's ruined—use it for heating fuel."

"It'll cost you too much to fix that problem."

"Use it for tomato stakes."

"Save the money and let me build you a new one from scratch."

Then my luck turned. I met Leo deMonbreun over the Internet.

The Fly Rod Chronicles

You've probably heard that cornball poem about an old violin that's being auctioned off for pennies? Then some old guy walks in, picks it up, tunes it, and plays this sweet ballad that makes everybody in the place go all gooey and weepy. The auctioneer starts the bidding again for *hundreds* of dollars.

Someone asks, "Why the change?"

Answer: the touch of the Master's hand.

Well, Leo is a true master rod builder. He has *the touch*. He sees value in old discarded sticks of bamboo. Leo can give new life to an old, nearly wrecked Rapidan. Not very often do such things (or people) get second chances.

Leo called to tell me that I had "won the lottery." I didn't understand what he meant. Then he explained: Years ago, the Montague Company mass-produced bamboo fly rods. They were partly built by hand, but most of the work was done by machines. The Rapidan was what's known as a "production" bamboo fly rod. But once in a great while, the people at Montague would get motivated to build a few rods from genuine Tonkin cane, by hand—just to prove they could still make a quality product. This rod was one of those few, handcrafted Tonkin cane rods.

I fish the Rapidan now, as often as time and conditions permit. At eight and a half feet, with both tips straightened and flame tempered; new guides, including an agate stripper; pretty orange and royal silks; a burled maple reel seat; and blued hardware, this rod is a masterpiece. The old gal spruced up quite nicely. Not only is it pretty to look at, it's now quite functional.

Restoring The Rapidan

It's a cannon: It can throw a #6 or #7 line with the best of the graphites; it does double, nay, triple duty. Streamers, nymphs, whatever. And the amazing thing? It can also cast a #22 BWO without any more splashdowns. It's almost like getting a heart transplant: There's a whole new life there.

I've had several people offer to buy it from me. No deal. Even though I now regularly buy, sell, and trade bamboo rods, I don't think I want to sell this one. There's too much history and nostalgia here.

No, I think I'll pass it on to my son. Even though he's not much of a bamboo guy now, maybe someday, after I'm gone, he'll take it out of the case, joint it up, waggle it a few times, and try to imagine the fish I caught with it. And he'll catch some good ones with it. And, with good care, he can pass it on to his son, Skyler. I believe it's really that good a rod.

Like all my rods, this one has a name.

It's called "Mark's Inheritance."

The Fly Rod Chronicles

CHAPTER 14

Fly Fishing Las Vegas

My business takes me to Las Vegas at least once a month, on average. Sometimes I fly; more often I drive. It's a six-hour drive, compared to the hassles of driving to the airport (half hour), parking and taking a shuttle into airport terminal (half hour). Then you check in, get your boarding pass, go through security check and wait for the plane (another hour or so, at least). The flight is another hour and a half. That's three and a half hours, so far. You get to Las Vegas; the plane taxis

The Fly Rod Chronicles

to your gate. You get off the plane and into the terminal. You stop and use the restroom; then you walk a half mile to the shuttle train. You take the little train into the main terminal, stand in line for a taxi or car rental, take the shuttle bus to the car rental; and, depending on which day of the week you arrive, it's almost another two hours before you're actually on the road to your hotel or appointments.

That's about five and a half hours of hassles, crowds, stress and exhaustion, compared to a leisurely drive that's mostly scenic, broken up by a stop in St. George for a meal, gas, and leg stretch. Along the way you might see deer or elk, maybe an eagle or two, and always a few hawks. There are some pretty mountain ranges, several nice small towns nestled up against the mountains, and many snug, trim-looking farms. There are a couple of stops where you can get some pretty decent country fried steak smothered in sausage gravy, with real home-made pie for dessert. ("You want that *with* a-la-mode, hon?")

I have another secret reason for my driving preference. Well, now it won't be a secret any more. I have a nifty little fly-fishing spot I can stop at along the way and get in anywhere from a half hour to a couple of hours fly fishing if I want.

My secret spot is about twenty miles off I-15, east of a small southern Utah town which shall remain nameless. It's a nice little freestone stream that flows out of a reservoir, through a twisting canyon of high, red, sandstone cliffs with Douglas firs and ponderosa pines, mixed with clumps of aspens, clinging to the slopes.

Fly Fishing Las Vegas

The stream itself flows through a bed of basalt boulders polished smooth by the water. The sides of the stream are shaded with occasional stands of willows, cottonwoods, alders, copper birch, and red twig dogwoods. The flora is sparse enough in most places that you can get a decent back cast free of hangups. The stream is close to the road, but that doesn't bother me; I've yet to see another fisherman on the stretch I fish, just a couple miles below the dam.

Because there is a dam, the water flow is controlled. Some techno-purists would say it's a *tailwate*r; because of the dam upstream the water temperature is fairly constant. I like to think of it more as a freestone stream, though.

From the dam downstream a couple miles, you can catch some nice rainbows in the twelve-to-sixteen-inch class. I think they're either hatchery trout the Utah Division of Wildlife Resources plants, or else escapees from the dam. Below that stretch for about another six miles or so, you'll find some very friendly browns. Most of the water, especially the downstream half from the dam, is accessible year round.

I'm remembering with fondness a recent whirlwind trip to Las Vegas. It was late October; it was still fairly warm in the desert. I was much in need of the cooling effects of my little stream and its surroundings. It beckoned me like an oasis.

I got away from Las Vegas about noon, fought my way through the mass of California gamblers pouring up I-15 from the south, north past the major turnoffs to The Strip, then past Downtown, through the Spaghetti Bowl, and north for the border.

The Fly Rod Chronicles

It was just barely three o'clock when I pulled off I-15 and drove slowly through the town, admiring several old authentic pioneer homes made of indigenous red sandstone. As I mentioned before, my son-in-law had an ancestor who settled the town in pioneer days. Someday I'll try to locate the old gentleman's original house.

Out to the east edge of town. I tried not to hurry as I drove up the winding, two-lane grade into the National Forest, keeping an eye out for free-range cattle.

A half hour, later I was in hip waders and vest and had my little seven-foot, three-weight bamboo rigged up with a 7x tippet. It's a sweet rod, the blank made by Jeff Fultz, on a Garrison 201 taper with two tips: a three- and a four-weight. My friend Leo deMonbreun had built the rod and finished it out beautifully. But not too beautifully to cause a case of nerves about fishing it; a nice blend of art and utility.

A splash of rising trout in the pool nearest the car park. Must be something hatching, but I don't see any bugs above the water. What fly to tie on? It was getting late, late afternoon shading on towards evening, but what the heck? I succumbed to the temptation to tie on a #18 Adams. It looked fairly buggy to me—the all-purpose buggy-looking fly. I hoped it looked buggy enough to these trout.

I chose a stretch of stream that was fairly straight, stair-stepping down the basalt rock formation. It reminded me very much of the famous Black Canyon of the Bear River in southern Idaho, where the lava flows created the same stair-step effect. Wide flat pools, where the water flows abruptly over the scarps in little, short falls; foam cover to hide trout; riffling down into another little plunge fall, over into the next pool. In this spot my little stream was a miniature model of Black Canyon.

A couple of false casts and the fly settled on the water, drifted a few inches with the slow current, then curled around a rock. Ping! A nice trout pounced on it and raced for the shadows. There was a lot of splashing and flashing in the small pool. I brought the fish to hand—a ten-inch brown, firm and still wiggling furiously, full of fight.

The trout released, I started to dress my fly, then had a thought. *I wonder?* I decided it would be fun to experiment and see how many *different* fly patterns they would hit before it got so dark I had to go. I switched to a #18 parachute Adams.

Next hole, new fly, similar results: a nice, fat, feisty ten-inch brown. This could prove to be fun. I clipped off the para Adams, and tied on a #20 Blue Winged Olive.

I took several steps upstream to another hole and cast the fly just to the left of some braided water, just below where it squirted through a sluice-like cleft in the rocks. An eager brownie took the fly and raced around the ten-foot pool in a frenzy. Totally uninhibited, I laughed out loud at his antics. This is good!

In turn, I tied on: a #20 para BWO, a #18 Pale Morning Dun; then a #20 thorax PMD. I caught a fish on each one— one fly, one fish! My own One Fly Contest. The trout were all about the same size, which I found interesting. Maybe some day I'll pursue the question of why they were all the same size.

But that day, it was getting dark and I needed to be on my way. I checked my watch. It was 4:55 p.m. I felt more relaxed than I had felt in ages. The road kinks were all gone from my neck. I hadn't had this much fun fishing in a long time. I was ready for the rest of the drive home.

CHAPTER 15

Teach A Man To Fish...

They say if you give a man a fish he eats for only one day; but if you *teach* him to fish...Well...

First, a friend introduces him to fly fishing, he loves it, and he has to buy:
- A bamboo rod (or two or three or four)
- A Peerless reel (or two or three or four)
- A technical fly line (or two or three or four)
- Breathable Gore-Tex waders

The Fly Rod Chronicles

- Breathable Gore-Tex "guide pants" waders (for the summer months)
- Neoprene waders (for winter fishing)
- Felt wading shoes
- Cleated wading shoes
- Wading sandals, for the summer months when he wades "wet"
- A wading staff
- A catch-and-release landing net
- A hundred dozen flies
- A driftboat
- A float tube
- Or, better yet, a kickboat, one that you can stand up in to cast
- An SUV to haul the driftboat and carry the float tube or kickboat, and all the gear
- A new, bigger vest to hold about twelve pounds of stuff (the old one ripped from the sheer weight of it all)
- A bigger SUV to carry all of the above
- A catch-and-release landing net with a retractable tape measure
- A lifetime membership in Trout Unlimited
- Excuses to fly places in order to rack up Frequent Flyer Miles to get him to Alaska next summer to fish that run of cohos with a new seven/eight-weight, eight-foot Paul H. Young River Guide model, bamboo fly rod
- A new Orvis large arbor reel to go with that new Paul Young River Guide rod

Teach A Man To Fish

- A few dozen more flies, designed especially with those Alaska cohos in mind
- A lifetime membership in the Henry's Fork Foundation
- A newer, better, tougher trailer for the driftboat
- A new burglar-proof safe (preferably with humidity controls) to keep all those valuable bamboo rods
- Books on fly fishing; fly-fishing DVDs; a subscription to the Outdoor Channel and about a dozen fly-fishing, travel, and fly-tying magazines

Then he takes up fly tying, and the basement family room looks like an aviary floor, sans all the poop.

- He buys several larger fly boxes for all the flies he's tied
- He buys a special kit to capture live insects from the stream so he can make authentic matches of the flies he ties "to the real thing"
- He quits voting Republican ("They refuse to remove the dams from steelhead and salmon rivers;" "They just don't care enough about the environment;" etc., etc.)
- He starts going to yard and garage sales looking for old bamboo fly rods to restore and sell on eBay, hoping that he just might be lucky and stumble upon a perfectly preserved E.C. Powell, or a Wes Jordan Orvis, or a Paul Young Perfectionist, or an F.E. Thomas, or a Granger,

or a Leonard, or a rare Phillipson, or a Winston, and so on...
- He starts buying fly-fishing photos, prints and paintings to hang on the walls all over the house
- He buys a lifetime membership in Federation of Fly Fishing
- He buys SCUBA gear so he can now catch the pupae and nymphal forms of underwater insects, so he can tie "the real thing"

Then he becomes just a little bit *sneaky*, like calling in sick to work at least once every week on average.

- Dozens of unsolicited catalogs clog the mailbox every week, all dealing with fly fishing, outdoor clothing and gear, deals on travel to exotic places, etc. (He's now on everyone's mailing list because he subscribes to so many fly-fishing magazines)
- He starts giving his wife expensive fly-fishing "stuff" (rods, reels, lines, etc.) as anniversary, birthday and Christmas gifts (knowing she won't ever use them)
- He quits voting Democrat ("All they do is *talk* about a clean environment")
- He starts replacing her antique Stiffel lamps with those carved, wooden jumping rainbows, browns, and brook trout ones
- The credit card balances start climbing because of all the fly-fishing stuff he has to buy from the catalogs

(not to mention the many expensive trips to great fly-fishing spots)
- He starts suggesting they take their annual family vacation to such "neat" places as the Kenai Peninsula, or Belize, or New Zealand, or Russia's Kamchatka River, or Patagonia ("They have very pretty rivers, dear...you could sit on the banks and read while I fish, or you could take lots of pictures of me catching huge trout..."), and so on...
- "Speaking of Christmas, how about this cute Santa Claus dressed as a fly fisherman ornament set for the tree, honey...?"
- He starts using a whole new vocabulary, like "silks," "tippets," "tapers," "double haul," "going barb-less," "mending the drag," "nymphing," "early morning rise," etc. and his wife begins to wonder: *Is there a mistress....?*
- He grows a moustache or beard and long hair (and occasionally skips showering)
- He shucks the suit and tie and starts wearing to the office zip-off cargo pants, desert boots and baggy casting shirts with lots of big pockets
- He quits voting at all
- He gets fired from his *real* job
- He's not worried about being fired: "I've decided we can all move to Alaska where I'll take a job as a fly-fishing guide..."
- He has to take three jobs to pay the alimony and child

The Fly Rod Chronicles

support; he has no time or energy left for fly fishing,

Now you have a feckless, no good, bona fide Trout Bum. Brilliant!

CHAPTER 16

Just An Average Fly Fisherman

I think of myself as just an *average* fly fisherman. Most of my fly fishing is within fifty miles of home on small to medium-size streams or lakes. A normal cast for me is thirty feet or less. I don't tie my own flies; I get the ten-bucks-for-a-dozen closeout deals at Sportsmen's Warehouse or Wal-Mart. A few times each season I'll catch and release some nice fish,

The Fly Rod Chronicles

say over seventeen inches. Most of the time, they're your usual eight- or nine-inch brookies, and twelve-inch rainbows or browns.

The exception to average is my tackle. I do invest more than an average sum in good rods, reels, and lines, just because I believe good equipment lasts longer; and that has proven true many times. And let's face it, a classic Leonard bamboo or a Winston or Sage graphite rod deserves a good quality reel and line.

So being just your average fly fisherman, if someone calls and offers you the chance to try some incredible fly fishing, where you can realize your fantasies of huge trout on a fly rod, you'd be crazy not to accept. Right?

I got such a call from Steve, one of my business associates in Toronto, saying he had booked a trip for two persons with a guide out of Campbell River, British Columbia, for three days of heli-fishing in early March. He couldn't make it and would I and a friend like to go in his place?

"Heli-what?" I asked.

"They fly you by helicopter into these incredible rivers in B.C., and you catch so many big sea-run Bull Trout (Dolly Varden) and cutts your arm falls off! Call this guy in Vancouver, he'll fill you in."

So I called "this guy" in Vancouver. Turns out "this guy," Brad Chappell, is an avid fly fisherman, too, and a successful stock broker.

Brad Chappell is anything but average. A cocky, grinning, movie star-handsome, hard-drinking, hard-swearing third-

Just An Average Fly Fisherman

generation Irish-Canadian, Brad is a devoted trout bum. We talked a couple times by phone and he filled me in on the plans. I was skeptical when he swore I'd be catching sea-run Bull Trout as big as ten pounds. The largest I'd ever caught in Alaska were about fifteen inches, maybe a pound and a half. I thought we were talking Tooth Fairy fishing when he added that the sea-run cutthroats could go as big as five or six pounds, too.

I had just a week to fill the other open slot, get ready, buy plane tickets, and so on. My first go-to guy was my son, Mark, a high school teacher in Rigby, Idaho, another dedicated trout bum. He had early spring baseball tryouts and couldn't make it. "Otherwise... gosh, wish I could go..."

I called a couple other guys I knew. Conflicts, etc., the usual put-offs. Finally I called Randy Simpson, my accountant. Right in the middle of tax season for him and a really long shot, but he quickly accepted. (Randy would never let a silly thing like client tax returns get in the way of great fly fishing with guaranteed big fish.)

A week later we boarded a flight to Seattle, where we rented a car and drove to Tsawassen to catch the last B.C. Ferry to Campbell River on Vancouver Island.

I had phoned ahead and talked to our host and guide, Clint Cameron, owner of The Dolphins Resort and Marina. I asked Clint what we needed to bring, what rods and line sizes we needed. Did we need waders? What kind, neoprene or Gore-Tex? He said we really didn't need to bring anything; he was totally equipped for any fisherman, rods, boots, rain gear, etc.

The Fly Rod Chronicles

But I wanted to try out a new six-weight, five-piece graphite travel rod, so I packed that, knowing he had plenty of backup rods and reels should I break mine.

Campbell River is well-known as a Mecca for serious salmon and steelhead fly fishermen. Clint was just the guy to show us the ropes. He's a third generation river guide, grew up on the rivers and ocean around Campbell River. Now he's the proud owner of Dolphins. I wondered if Clint's and Brad's granddads were chums of the legendary Roderick Haig-Brown? Brad confirmed later that, indeed, they were.

It was late and raining when we pulled in. Clint met us, made us feel welcome and offered a late night cold lunch. We would set off at seven-thirty in the morning, so we ate and got to bed. I fell asleep in a warm down bed, listening to the lonely sounds of ships' horns in the night as they traversed the narrow ocean passage that runs adjacent to Dolphins Resort.

We had a huge breakfast of hotcakes, eggs, bacon, the usual. The peaceful atmosphere was suddenly interrupted by the whapping sound of an approaching helicopter. We quickly finished the last of our meal, and piled our stuff into the bright yellow Avistar that had landed on a pad just twenty yards from our dining room on a narrow, gravelly spit near the water.

We were then introduced to Rado, a friendly, highly competent helicopter pilot. The name "Rado" (pronounced ray-dough) was short for something Hungarian that I never did quite catch. Didn't matter; we were soon on our way, four of us crammed into the back seat, and one lucky guy riding shotgun.

Just An Average Fly Fisherman

Our route took us northeast, across the narrow Straights, past the northern tip of Vancouver Island, then inland several miles over ancient glaciers and massive ice fields. We were stunned by the magnificent aerial view. We saw eagles on every little island or land point: bald, golden, and ospreys, too. As we came over the mainland, we spotted a family of mountain goats feeding among the crags.

Our first day of fishing would put us on a small, glacial river, a milky jade green, flowing steadily, but not too swift to wade. Rado settled his bird down on a broad sandbar created by millennia of spring floods. Sand flew and swirled in small whirlwinds until the rotors stopped and I stepped out into the frosty air. It was March 1 at nine a.m.

My hands shook as I jointed and lined up my new travel rod. I don't know if it was the cold or excitement, but I pretty soon calmed down as I chose my spot on the river and made a few false casts. On Brad's advice, I tied on a #8 olive woolly booger (for cultural reasons I won't go into here, Canadians prefer to call them wooly "boogers," rather than *buggers*.)

I was told this kind of fishing was much like fly fishing for salmon in Alaska. That is, cast across and up, let the fly sink and dead drift downstream with rod tip following, pulling in slack line. When your fly is straight downstream from you, give it the classic Leisenring Lift, slowly; watch the line and if you feel or see any tightness, even the slightest, set the hook with a steady pull, not a jerking strike.

And that's exactly what happened on my first cast. I was soon into a lively Bull Trout. It fought just like a brown, I thought, including the head wagging and rolling on the gravelly bottom. I hauled in slack line, got it on the reel, and played it almost five minutes before it tired enough for me to slowly reel it in to the net. It didn't give up easily.

My first sighting of the fish, as it rolled over on the surface, was impressive. It had to be six to seven pounds, and at least twenty-two inches. The sun had broken through the cloud cover and the silver and pink sides flashed and glistened like a tarpon's coloring. I admired the large peach-colored spots on its sides that identify it as Dolly Varden.

Clint came over and helped with the net. He congratulated me, then yelled out to the other guys, "First fish!"

Before leaving the resort we had agreed on some bets: first fish; biggest, smallest, prettiest, ugliest, etc., all at five dollars each betting category. A fistfight almost erupted over whether to issue Canadian dollars (Randy and I dubbed them "nano dollars.") or American greenbacks. The majority finally agreed on U.S. dollars as the currency for settling debts.

On the phone the week before, Brad had explained the mystery of the sea-run part. He said Mother Nature was telling the billions of little salmon fry that had hatched in the fall that now was the time to go out to sea and grow up. Mother Nature was also telling the dollies and cutts out in the ocean it was time for them to run upstream for a buffet lunch of little salmon fry. Everybody's happy, see? Especially me, Mr. Average Fly Fisherman, who now looked like an expert. The big mystery to me was, how did the dollies and cutts adapt so quickly to fresh water? I'll have to research that one.

Just An Average Fly Fisherman

We fished the first location for about an hour, during which time Clint and Rado revved up the Avistar and scouted other locations. They returned, we stowed our rods, still strung up, under the belly of the copter in a specially designed rod rack; we squeezed into our seats, buckled in, and flew on to a new location that was loaded with more fish.

As it turned out, the contest soon became academic. We were catching too many fish and having too much fun to keep track. When we finally took a break for a gourmet picnic lunch, somebody asked if anyone was keeping count. We pretty much agreed it had been a twenty-five-fish morning for everyone, mostly dollies, and a couple of cutts, even though this particular river was not known for its cutthroat run. Clint seemed surprised at the cutts. The biggest Dolly was an eight-pounder Brad's friend had caught. The favored fly pattern? Just about anything in the streamer group that looked remotely like a young salmon fry: all colors of woolly *boogers*, but olive seemed to be the most effective; Clousers, Zonkers, bunny and leech patterns, you name it, they were hitting.

It struck me this kind of fishing was designed for average fly fishermen like me: It took away the stress of having to match the hatch when a rise was on. Sure, I like to catch trout on dry flies more than almost anything; but I was going to milk this dream trip for all the happiness I could get out of it. These chances don't come around very often for guys like me.

#

The Fly Rod Chronicles

That afternoon went pretty much the same as the morning. The shadows were lengthening in the narrow valley; the sun was glowing golden off the snowy peaks nearby. It was about four-thirty when Clint said we ought to be going, while Rado had the advantage of daylight. We were a bunch of reluctant, but happy, anglers when we boarded for the ride back.

But the day was not yet over. Clint has a tradition of having Rado stop the chopper atop a glacier-covered mountain peak for a few minutes before the final lap home. The mountain-top celebration comes complete with vintage wine chilled in snow and cigars with the guests. What a breathtaking view we had from 12,000 feet! I could spot the Lions of North Vancouver about eighty miles south. The lichen-spotted rocks on our landing spot were old (I wondered at their age). Besides our party, I wondered how many men had ever set foot on this peak. Any ancient indigenous tribes?

For a few choice moments I felt at peace. I felt darn lucky to be there watching the flaming sunset among friends.

Clint came up to me, stood alongside, and said "Ever see anything more beautiful?"

"Yes, the birth of a child," I said.

He nodded.

Back at the resort, we dined on fresh salmon with dill sauce, had a dip in the hot tub. Then I crashed, replaying in my mind, over and over, hearing the swish of the taut line through milky jade-green water; the strikes, the bend of the rod, the dogfight, the flash of silvery sides as the fish gave up

Just An Average Fly Fisherman

and turned on the surface.

Our first day turned out sunny and bright; but day two was cold, with low-hanging clouds and that constant, light misty-drizzle for which the Northwest is famous. The kind that somehow soaks into your skin and chills you even if you have heavy weather protection. But it was the perfect day for fly fishing: Fish get bolder when it's cloudy, especially when there's rain dappling the surface.

We fished a different river than the first day. The first thing I noticed was how much it reminded me of the South Fork of the Snake: freestone cobble rocks, with lots of long, flat runs interspersed with riffles pouring over gravel bars. Lots of cut-banks and logjams. Perfect spots for fish to lie resting, protected beneath the roiling foamy braids and spills, content to let the food come to them. It appeared wade-able, and it was in most places. The water was clear compared to the milky, jade-green river from the day before. (I think here I need to tell the reader that we all made a solemn promise to Clint we would never reveal the names of the two rivers. So don't make me lie to you to protect my sources.)

The first day was mostly Bull Trout fishing. Clint promised we'd be getting into more sea-run cutthroats today. The fly patterns and the technique would be the same, but the fish would take the fly and fight differently, I would soon learn.

My first fish in the first hole came quickly, on the first cast. A good omen. I was surprised at the weight of this fish, which took a pearl Zonker eagerly. Another Dolly, judging from the brown trout-like way it bore down to the bottom, shaking its head angrily. I played it for about five minutes before bringing it to the net. A silvery, ten-pounder, the biggest I had hooked so far. I grinned as Clint snapped my picture.

I released the fish, dressed my fly and sharpened the hook. I flung the Zonker up and across the run, watching it sink quickly as it drifted downstream. Before the fly got halfway downstream from me, I saw the line tighten. I counted to three, and set the hook deep into the jaw of the first guy's bigger, meaner brother.

He surprised me by shooting up to the surface, rolling and splashing a mere fifteen feet away. I was stripping in slack line as fast as my cold fingers could work. In a few seconds, I had him on the reel. Then he got bugged at the pressure he was feeling in his jaw and shot downstream, stripping out line, the reel screaming, almost smoking, making music to my ears. He was headed straight for a mass of dead wood stacked on the outside of the bend. I prayed the reel could take this stress. My rod was almost bent double as I fought to turn him; I was already into the backing.

The pressure turned him and he fought me every foot as I slowly gained line: pumping, reeling, pumping, reeling…He shot up to the surface, rolling on top. He was huge! As he dove for the bottom again, I experienced the sickening feeling of the line going slack, no angry weight, no pressure. Nothing. Not even my fly. The knot had finally loosened from the stress and he pulled free; no broken leader. I had tied on a good clinch knot; it just worked loose from stress.

I stood stunned for a couple minutes, shaking from the

Just An Average Fly Fisherman

cold, breathing heavily from the fight.

"Too bad," Clint consoled. "He looked like a big'un."

I tied on a chartreuse-and-black Clouser, making really sure the knot was more secure this time. It took a couple of casts and drifts, but then I struck and hooked into a new fish. He jumped a couple times and I knew it wasn't a Dolly. A couple minutes later, I netted my first cutt of the day, about four pounds and silvery bright, a chromer, fresh from the cold Pacific.

After pictures and a careful release I checked the leader knot and sharpened my hook. Satisfied I was ready, I cast and let the fly drift. I saw the line stretch and stop. I raised my wrist about three inches vertically, and instantly knew I was into another big fish. It had to be a Dolly. It was.

The fish shot to the surface and rolled. Déjà vu? As the big Dolly rolled, I saw a slash of red in its mouth, then he dove for the bottom. Was I mistaken? Was it a huge cutt instead? The mist had increased to a soft drizzle; my glasses were so messed up I could have easily been mistaken. No time to stop and clean them. Not an inch of dry cloth on me anyway.

I stayed with that big guy for almost twenty minutes before he finally gave up the fight and rolled onto his side. As I brought him to the net, he rolled over to his other side, revealing the red gash I thought was either cutty markings or blood. That was no cutty and that was no blood. It was my pearl Zonker, the one with a bit of red flash tied in it!

Another photo of a smiling me holding up a huge Dolly that weighed in at twelve pounds! Was I ecstatic? Me, the

The Fly Rod Chronicles

Average Fly Fisherman, now King of the World!

I released Captain Zonker from the fish's mouth, and released the big fish back into the river. I stabbed the battered fly into my hat band. He'd earned a well-deserved retirement. It's still stuck in my hat band to this day.

All too quickly, that trip was over, as dream trips like this are. I had a lot of nice pictures to look at and even more memories of catching all those great fish. High on my list is the promise to myself of a return trip some day.

Now whenever I'm feeling generally down, or maybe below par after a day of poor fishing, I only have to look at those pictures or that "Captain Zonker" fly in my hat to bring back sweet memories of the two days when I was king of all fly fishermen.

CHAPTER 17

Band Of Brothers

Part II

I had had over two years to consider what happened in the First Annual Submarine Race, as Fred dubbed it. Jim circulated an e-mail in late October inviting all of us to another "Bro-union." I accused them of conspiring to drown me a second time, since they had botched the first attempt.

There's never a convenient time; but the weekend following Thanksgiving was agreed on and I started making

The Fly Rod Chronicles

plans. Elvan wanted to join in but was a little short of funds, what with Christmas coming and being between jobs. I offered to take him if he'd help me drive.

This time would be different, very different. First, we were joined by one more brother who didn't make the Idaho trip, Paul, age 52, now single, a high school economics teacher. Second, we'd be meeting at Jim and Fred's in Chicago on a Sunday, then transfer over to a small town in Southern Michigan, Berrien Springs. (Turns out some of our ancestors came from there.) We'd fish only one day for steelhead, Monday, on the St. Joseph's River.

As we pulled into Berrien Springs Sunday evening just at dusk, Fred insisted we drive down to see the river and marina before we bought licenses and checked in to our motel. As we looked at the quiet, dark water, Fred said chances were we might even hook into some walleyes, browns, even Chinook salmon, as well as the steelhead. To prove it was fishy, Fred had plenty of photos from prior steelheading trips on this river with the same captain we had chartered.

The St. Joe's reminded me a lot of the Sacramento River where we grew up. Maybe the Sacramento reminded our forbears of the St. Joe's when they came west to northern California during in the Gold Rush.

The area around Berrien Springs is typical of so many upper-Midwest small towns. A central part of town, complete with crossroads, brick courthouse, a large church or two and a park; many trim, sturdy homes; and the town surrounded by rolling, hilly country, with deep, dark, rich soil. Open fields stretched everywhere, interspersed with small farms, fruit orchards now dormant, stands of pine and hardwoods.

The main farming activity now seemed to be vineyards and wineries. But there remained many old fruit orchards scattered around, mostly apple, but a few peach and cherries also. I closed my eyes and imagined it in spring, when the grass was new and the orchards in full blossom.

Winding its way silently through this pastoral scene was the St. Joe's, flowing westward beneath steep banks toward mighty Lake Michigan, ultimately to emerge somewhere at the mouth of the Saint Lawrence, then to the Atlantic Ocean.

It was Elvan's fiftieth birthday, so we had to celebrate. A local Mexican restaurant came highly recommended. I'm usually suspect of anything Mexican east of Denver, but this place proved to be pretty good. (For half our gang, well-lubricated with Margaritas, I don't think the food mattered.)

At any rate, we all had a good time; the serving staff serenaded Elvan with a Mexican happy birthday song, served him fried ice cream with one candle, and presented him with a huge, silly sombrero. Two of the brothers sang a drunken rendition of some other Mexican tune; I didn't recognize any of the words. Elvan accepted it all in good humor.

Afterward, we hung around Fred's room for several hours telling stories of the good (and not-so-good) old days, some of the guys doing their best to kill a bottle of Crown Royal. Nobody made a move to go to bed. I think we really enjoyed the brief time being together again, having fun, being boys.

I asked Fred about the fishing we'd be doing the next day.

The Fly Rod Chronicles

His good friend, Captain Gary ran a charter/guide service out of the marina we'd checked out on our arrival. Fred had booked us with Captain Gary DeRosa's Goldeneye Charters. Fred was the veteran; he'd fished here many times over several years. In fact, a picture of his wife Sue, hefting a nice Chinook salmon, is featured in Gary's color brochure.

We were up at 4:45; well, at least the alarm went off then. I finally dragged my grumpy body out about 5:10 when Jim threatened to leave me behind.

I was impressed with the license-buying process they have in Michigan. Michigan Division of Natural Resources (MDNR) requires that you buy a lifetime "sport card" for a mere buck. You have to carry it with your valid fishing or hunting license. If your name or address changes, you simply buy a new sport card. The 24-hour non-resident fishing license was another eight dollars. That's it. Then you're in their computer for the next time, and there will be a next time.

We made the usual five dollar bets: first fish, biggest, most, smallest, ugliest, etc. But this time I insisted we name each fish, just for fun. We also made sure everyone used the toilet at the boat basin. Mexican food does funny things and the pontoon boats we'd be fishing on did *not* look like they had onboard commodes.

We all introduced ourselves to our two captain/guides, Gary and Barry. They were amazed there were so many guys with the same last name but soon understood we were all brothers. We divided up—the four brothers on Barry's boat were Jim, Elvan, Bobby, and me; while Fred, Joe, and Paul

Band Of Brothers – Part II

were on Captain Gary's boat. We hopped on board the two enclosed, heated pontoon craft. It was still very dark when we cast off, Gary heading upstream toward the dam, and we went downstream. Our captain, Barry, was very much at ease with steering this craft in the dark, which also put me at ease enough to catch a quick nap beside the onboard kerosene stove. .

After about twenty minutes of careful cruising, we pulled close to the far bank and dropped anchor. Other than the hissing of the kerosene stove, the only sound was the lapping and gurgling of the current against the pontoons as the boat slowly rocked.

I quickly took a liking to Barry, our guide. He was stocky, yet agile, with a quiet, efficient, no-nonsense manner. His grizzled, gruff appearance was softened somewhat by his thick glasses.

Barry gathered us around and explained we'd be using several eight-foot Browning casting rods, Abu-Garcia casting reels strung with ten-pound Trilene mono. Six rods stood at attention on the stern; we would be using fresh roe as bait, weighted and bounced as close to the bottom as possible. The two outrigger rods would be trolling a silver and red Bomber-looking lure.

He demonstrated the technique of "walking" the bait, paying out line until he was sure it was touching bottom. We were all to keep alert, keep an eye on as many rods as we could manage. If there was a "bite," he would set the hook, and then hand the rod to the nearest fisherman. Thereafter, we'd rotate turns playing a fish, should we be so lucky.

The Fly Rod Chronicles

The problem of figuring out honors for first fish was solved with walkie-talkies between the two boats; the two guides kept in constant contact anyway: sharing information about location, how many bites, actual catches, species, what bait/lure, depths, etc. Sounded to me a lot like the chatter you hear on trout streams between guides and their clients, only more high tech.

We hung around the first spot almost half an hour; nothing happening, so we pulled anchor and moved to a new spot. Barry said the steelies, fresh from Lake Michigan, favored hugging the banks, or lying just below riffles, or in deeper holding pools.

The second spot brought no bites, so we pulled anchor and moved again. It was now daylight and close to eight o'clock; nothing to panic about; after all, steelheads are called "the fish of a thousand casts." The quiet was broken by wild turkeys clacking and calling on a nearby oak-covered island.

I've been steelheading twice before, so I knew how frustrating this kind of fishing can be. The first time was in late February 2003, on Vancouver Island's Gold River with Randy Simpson the day before we tied into the sea-run Bull Trout and cutties. I didn't actually keep count (who could), but I swear from the ache in my arms and shoulders I cast a thousand times for just one single "bump" on that prior outing.

The second time was in October, the year—well, in fact, the same day—the Yankees took Boston in Game One. I fished only an hour on the Yuba River with my good friend,

Band Of Brothers – Part II

Dale Wilder. It's a secret spot and I'm sworn not to reveal the location. But if I told you, you'd say, "No way!"

That morning I caught one small steelie on my third cast. It was only sixteen inches long, but was all attitude and fought like a barracuda. It was my first steelie and I'll always remember it. And I took it using my restored Montague Rapidan with a Silver Hilton lead fly with one of Ron Sharp's Blue Zulus as a dropper. The fish took the dropper... But I digress...

#

Our first "bite" on the St. Joe's came at exactly 8:03 a.m. It was now daylight and I could easily see the tip of rod #1—baited with fresh roe—the farthest on the left, bend and jerk in that familiar way of a fish taking.

"Fish on!" I shouted. I was actually the closest, but I deferred so Bobby could be the first. Barry struck and the fish broke the surface: a beautiful, fresh "chromer." Then he passed off the rod so Bob could take over. With encouragement from us and coaching from Barry, Bobby was able to bring it to net.

Being a believer of catch and release, it really bothered me when Barry administered last rites. Bobby was one proud dude as he posed for pictures. It looked about twenty-four inches and probably hefted around six and a half pounds, a female.

Then came the naming. Bobby named it Claude, starting

a trend for all our fish that day to bear effeminate French boy (*petits hommes*) names. At the Mexican dinner the night before, I'd caught several ribbings about my wife being a high school French teacher. I had jokingly suggested we find a French restaurant (as if there *were* any in this small town), instead of Mexican. Loud guffaws, but that phrase, "We are French, you know," stuck around all the next day. It became one of those code phrases we will wear out in the future, sort of like the *P-flueger* reel thing.

The kidding was momentarily interrupted when Captain Barry got a call on his cell phone—a buddy trying to line him up on a date with a lady from Kalamazoo. After Barry finished the phone call, he wired in to Captain Gary; turns out their boat caught the first fish at 7:55 a.m.

About then, Elvan got his turn at landing a fish, a two-and-a-half pound walleye. He took it in good humor, when we assured him that fish was guaranteed to take both smallest and ugliest fish honors. Someone suggested he was exempt from naming it since it already came with a name: UGLY!

But Barry took exception to our joking. "They're really a damn good eatin' fish," he said.

I asked him how he liked to cook walleyes.

"Chunks in beer batter, deep fried."

"Steelhead, too?"

"Yep. Everything. Same way—it's the best."

"Do you ever smoke them—steelies?"

"Yeah, they're okay."

"Something you like better?"

Band Of Brothers – Part II

"Smoked chubs."

There followed that period of polite silence in which nobody can think of anything to say that would be politically correct. I decided then and there to christen his boat the SS Chub; for obvious reasons, I kept the name to myself. Barry was a former apple farmer; I don't think he had any patience for smart asses, even if the smart ass *is* a paying client.

#

By around nine o'clock, we had moved several more times. The temperature was quickly dropping close to freezing; a breeze whipped up and a soft mist began to fall. I retreated into the cabin and huddled near the kerosene heater.

About one-thirty we shared our lunch with Barry: convenience store ham salad sandwiches, chips, warm Pepsis. Barry thanked us and suggested we go back to where we caught the first steelie. Captain Gary radioed in: They caught a large walleye and lost two nice steelhead.

We were hardly anchored in the original lucky spot with the lines out when we got a "bite." It was Jim's turn and he netted a nice female chromer a little bigger than Bob's. We had barely removed the hook, taken pictures, and named her (Jeanne-Pierre—a man's name!), when the next bite came. My turn.

I learned something new about fishing that day: Keep the rod tip *down* to control the fish when it's in close around the boat. I was used to keeping my fly-rod tip *up* when playing a fish on a stream or lake. Barry only yelled at me once; I managed to keep my cool and not retort in kind. I landed my first *big* steelhead. I kissed it, posed with it for pictures and turned away so I didn't have to see it killed. It measured twenty-eight inches long, fourteen-inch girth, and weighed a hair under eight pounds. A female, bright with red gills and pinkish sides, fresh, and full of roe. Barry was happy about the fresh roe.

I still don't understand why they insist on killing all of the fish that are caught. I told Barry I wanted to release it; he got a really funny look in his eyes, like maybe he suspected I had voted for John Kerry or something.

Also, he had a Weapon of Mass Destruction in his hand and he was pretty skilled at using it. Hey, it's their boat, their rules. When he comes out West we'll do it *my* way. (I named her Guy, pronounced "Gee," the French way.)

It was nearly two-thirty; we were scheduled to pull off the river at three o'clock. Not much time left for Elvan to score with his steelie. It wasn't looking too good.

Barry turned around and cruised us upriver, about a hundred yards past the boat basin, then dropped anchor for the last time. We were in a fairly fast-running channel, hugging the far bank; the earthen bank rose up about thirty feet above us. We were close enough to the bridge to almost make out the eye coloring of the car passengers. Captain Gary stopped his boat near ours on his way in and traded news and river boatmen talk for a minute, then he left us alone.

Elvan stood on the fantail, hands in pockets, looking

Band Of Brothers – Part II

downstream, smiling yet stoic, while Barry tended lines. The rest of us were inside trying to warm up, when I commented, "Wouldn't it be so sweet if Elvan could hook one right now?"

No sooner spoken than I saw a rod tip plunge down. I think we all three saw it at the same time, because, "Fish on!" was a chorus.

Fish hooked. Fish played. Fish killed and named: Yves.

Final score: Fred caught first and biggest; his nudged my weight by about six ounces and one inch in length (I was happy for him—he managed this in spite of his crippling arthritis). Elvan caught most (two), smallest and ugliest. We all felt bad for Joe; he didn't catch anything, although he had one steelie on and lost it.

"Just wait until next time," he said and grinned.

I was happy and revived; a successful trip.

And at least they didn't drown me—the feckless cowards didn't even try!

The Fly Rod Chronicles

CHAPTER 18

Menu Fishing

When I was a kid, I used to get a high out of sneaking onto private property to fish. But I always had this moral dilemma: My parents taught me to respect private property—always ask first. The other side was the temptation (really the *thrill*) to get away with something that was marginally wrong. Okay, it *was* wrong.

I admit I always felt a little guilty about the fish I caught and took home from other people's streams, sort of like stealing watermelons or corn. But, darn it, the people who owned that beautiful mile-long stretch of Berry Creek that meandered through a pretty meadow (my first real spring-creek experience), were city folk who only came up to the mountains a couple of times each summer. I reckoned I was doing them a favor by thinning out the fish population so the trout wouldn't crowd each other out of existence. I never let on to my parents what I was doing, and I didn't do it on a regular basis, either; which I guess made it more okay. Sort of.

I also justified my actions by telling myself I had a good precedent for what I was doing, right there in my own family tree. My dad's father had a reputation for being a meat hunter. This was in the early part of the Twentieth Century before real efforts and laws about game management came into being. He shot deer, wild hogs, ducks and geese near Marysville, California (sometimes out of season), selling the meat to some fancy Sacramento hotels through the back door. So I had a genetic defect that favored poaching, I guess you might say.

We grew up so poor that even our patches had patches on them. If I told you some of the conditions I lived in as a kid, you wouldn't believe me anyway. You'd probably say I was making it all up, or stealing stories from some Dickens novel.

So I guess I grew up with this awful sense of wanting to belong, to be invited to the neat parties the rich kids gave, which never happened. It sucks standing on the outside, looking in while someone else is having all the fun.

Menu Fishing

It didn't make me bitter; I just compensated by practicing woodcraft, hunting, trapping and fishing whenever I could, doing it my way, sometimes with just a few choice buddies, sometimes with one, sometimes by myself. I comforted myself with the knowledge I could survive in the wilds, but I bet those rich kids sure as heck couldn't.

I had day-dreams, visions of some spoiled fat kid, wetting his pants and crying for his momma, curling into a ball, waiting for Death's arrival. Meanwhile, I would be busy making a lean-to and bed out of fir boughs, rustling up food, and building a cozy fire. I'd sit and wait, all right, but it wouldn't be for Death. I'd amuse myself with getting straight in my mind my survival story for all to hear when I got "rescued" later:

LOCAL BOY FOUND IN GOOD SHAPE IN COZY CAMP AFTER SEVEN DAYS LOST IN MOUNTAIN WILDERNESS, the headlines would read in papers as far away as San Francisco. Pretty soon, I was sure, my Dad would come whistling along, praising me for the fine camp I'd made. Well, that (and others like it) was a pretty good fantasy; it kept my psyche healthy through a lot of rejection.

Weekends and vacations were for being outdoors, and I admit I spent a lot of time outside. Suited me fine; I loved it outdoors. It's still where I'd rather be any time.

Fast forward about twenty-some years to when I was in my mid-thirties. I was then in private law practice and a new client from Calgary (who appeared to be as rich as Daddy Warbucks) invited me goose hunting one September. Boy was I excited about this trip. This was to be no ordinary, let's-

The Fly Rod Chronicles

set-up-some-decoys-out-in-the-Alberta-cornfields type of shooting. No siree!

First, his corporate jet picked me up and flew me to Calgary. On the way, I got to use the onboard telephone, a first. I was offered sandwiches (without crusts) by an officious steward (I didn't mind his snobiness; I was having a great old time). We spent the night in Calgary, in comfort. Then next day, after a to-die-for breakfast, we picked up a couple of other rich guys, my client's buddies. Next we flew across the continent to Toronto, where we picked up a couple more rich guys, more of my client's pals. We landed that night in Timmins, Ontario, site of one of the most famous mines in the world. It was fun to actually see the mine that was the site of a major case in securities law, insider trading and fraud, a case I had studied in law school.

We spent the night in a nifty old hotel, nice dinner of Alberta beef steaks, salad, baked potatoes, and cheesecake for dessert. The dinner was designed by my client as a social function to introduce everyone who didn't already know each other. It turned out this group was a veritable Who's Who of Canadian Industry and Finance: I met the chairman and president of the largest bank in Canada, the president of a huge casualty insurance company (maybe the biggest in Canada); the president of a Canadian aircraft manufacturer, and the president of Elf Aquitaine Canada (a gracious Frenchman based in Montreal). It also turned out my shooting partner was my client's company counsel, a young lawyer about my age. This young lawyer's name was being put forward for

Menu Fishing

QC honors (Queen's Counsel). "Taking silk" was a pretty big deal, I learned.

I pinched myself. For the next five days I'd be shooting alongside these guys doing Guy Stuff: playing poker at night for matchsticks, scratching in secret places, belching, cussing at missed shots, and, yes, sitting in one side of the two-holer with them.

Next morning, we loaded onto an old DC-3 and pounded our way north for several hours, skimming just a couple hundred feet above the tundra, finally bouncing down on a gravel strip in the bush. Location: James Bay, Canada.

I could fill several pages describing this outstanding trip of a lifetime. Suffice that I came back home with a new perspective on the *good life*. Oh, the possibilities if one were rich! I was convinced that money *could* buy a better quality of outdoor experiences. I was also convinced that it wasn't so much the amount of money spent, but the quality of the experience that mattered most.

In the entire week we spent together, shooting our limits of geese every day, the only discussions about money I heard from these obviously powerful, wealthy guys, was one question to Samuel, one of our Cree Indian guides:

How much did a single 12-gauge shotgun shell cost way up here in the bush? (Answer at that time: one Canadian dollar.) Other than that, they wore the same faded blue jeans, flannel shirts, broken-in hunting boots as I did. They got tired, cold and wet the same as I did. They got hungry and thirsty and developed heartburn from too much good food, same as

The Fly Rod Chronicles

I did.

But I also relearned what I'd learned as a boy: Money could get them the choicest of hunting and fishing camps and guides. I learned that these guys hunted elk, moose and pheasants together; they fished for salmon and steelhead in British Columbia together, and so on. It was obvious they liked each other, that they got along famously, like good friends would who were comfortable with each other's outdoor manners and ethics. They knew each other could be trusted not to cheat at cards or slip whiskey to the Cree guides (a serious offense up there in the bush).

I went on the trip with a strong negative bias from my blue-collar upbringing that went something like this: If you have to pay to hunt or fish on a property, somehow it isn't an authentic outdoors activity, the genuine kind that my dad and uncles and granddads enjoyed. The democratic, people's kind of bias that had been indoctrinated into me.

Over the course of many more years, however, I have come to appreciate any chance to be out hunting or fishing, whether it's on public or private land. I treat the land the same, no matter where I am, because the rules, after all, are the same everywhere. Now I ask permission to fish on somebody else's land; I pick up after myself; I pick up other people's trash. I lock gates. I'm careful I don't wreck things crossing fences. I'm especially careful with fire and fire pits. I buy my license the first of January; I scrupulously observe the fish and game laws. And I say thank you to the guy who lets me fish on his property.

Menu Fishing

#

Another important thing I've come to appreciate is the value of a good guide. Now there's something that can cost some *real* dollars. I have a fly-fishing friend who doesn't believe in guides; he'd rather figure out a river or stream or lake for himself. That's okay, if that's your preference.

But, at my age, every precious minute counts. I'd rather pay a guide to get me to the best locations in the most efficient way. I'd like someone who knows the water, is especially good in a driftboat; knows the peculiar hazards of his river (cf. South Fork Landerman Brothers Reunion, 2002), etc. I like to know he's a good oarsman, a good river man. My life is in his hands, and I want to feel safe.

He'll also know the insect hatches, the cycles, best times of day to fish, and so on. I don't mind if my guide suggests I cast just behind that big, red rock over there. He probably knows a big trout or two live there, probably knows them by name. Okay with me.

These guys are professionals; they spend the better part of their lives out on the water, working on their melanoma; most of them trying their hardest to give their client all they paid for. And I truly believe a good guide, as a professional, is worth every dollar they get.

One of my most memorable experiences was a pay-as-you-go fishing outing a couple summers ago, when time was short and Mark and I were trying to figure how to squeeze in some fun float-tube fishing in just one afternoon. This was to be my first outing with a new belly boat, so I was a little apprehensive about trying any water that was difficult.

The guide suggested we try a local lake. He almost apologized when he said they charged a rod fee. Since this was to be my first time with a float tube, a friendly, family-type lake sounded pretty safe to me. It also sounded less intimidating, since the real professional float-tubers would be out on Henry's Lake and I wouldn't have to worry about how clumsy and inexperienced I looked. I was perfectly okay with the rod fee thing, which turned out to be reasonable.

The lake, about forty or so acres in size, was stocked with rainbows and small mouth bass. The owner went over the situation with us. No license necessary since this was private land. Rainbows were sulking on the bottom due to the recent hot weather; probably wouldn't catch any. If we did catch any trout, we should land them fast and release them carefully, trying to not stress them too much. If we should catch an eighteen-inch small mouth, bring it to him and our outing was free. He wanted a "big'un" to hang on the wall, sort of a PR gimmick. Otherwise, barbless hooks and catch-and-release, got all that? We did.

We rigged up our rods and inflated our belly boats. Then we hiked about a quarter of a mile around the lake to a stand of cottonwood trees, packing our float tubes over our shoulders. There was a nice rocky point adjacent to the trees, with shaded water; we figured that's where the bass would most likely be. Keep in mind this was also the first time fly fishing for small

Menu Fishing

mouth bass for me.

We started in around two o'clock. The day was sunny, warm but not sweltering, with a lot of big, puffy thunderclouds on the western horizon. We agreed that if it started raining seriously, we'd get off the water fast. We'd heard of too many true stories of dead fishermen, killed when lightning struck their graphite rods. At Mark's suggestion, I left my eight-foot bamboo back at the house this time, in favor of a longer graphite rod that would work better for casting from a belly boat.

Mark suggested we tie on flesh-colored bunny leeches and just paddle along, drifting the flies deep behind us, using sinking tip lines, sort of trolling along. We did this about twenty yards out from the banks for almost half an hour without any hits. We were in deeper water. From all the literature I'd read up on small mouth bass, it seemed we were too far out. I remembered reading that small mouths tend to hang out in shallower weedy or rocky areas.

I paddled myself in closer and cast to the bank, let the fly sink, and started a slow, jerking retrieve. About two jerks and I got my first hit. I set and he dove for the bottom, acting every bit like a brown trout. I glanced over and Mark also had one on. I let out a yip and brought the fish in to me. It was about twelve inches, maybe a pound and a half, all attitude. I admired it up close, trying to see for myself if it really did have a bronze back and red eyes. It did. *Are their eyes always that way, or do they turn red when frightened or angry? Maybe some expert can tell me some day.* I released it and went back

The Fly Rod Chronicles

for more.

We caught and released about a dozen more fish each, all about the same size. A wind came up and I saw a heavy, dark cloud cover about a mile away, scudding toward us fast. I could also see a gray wall of rain on the leading edge of the clouds. I called to Mark and pointed at the approaching storm.

"Let's pull out!" I shouted.

Figuring it would pass by us quickly, we opted to wait out the storm by just sitting in the shallows with our rods down.

The wall of rain hit the south end of the lake and ripped toward us. We were in it soon, getting drenched, but it was only cool, not cold— but refreshing.

I learned that when you're out on the water in a belly boat there's a much different dimension to sensations all around you, such as sound, which gets magnified. For instance, before the short storm, we could hear conversations of people at the campground several hundred yards away, almost as clearly as if we were up close. Large, flat bodies of water must be some kind of sound transmitter. I don't really know.

Also, your perspective of the world around you changes dramatically. You're down low on the water, looking up at most everything around you. You're almost eye level with the fish you catch. Much different from the fisherman's crouch— bending down from a standing position alongside a stream.

From that low perspective, almost eye level with the water, we saw the most marvelous, natural sight I think I have ever seen. The sunlight came breaking through the heavy rain

Menu Fishing

clouds for about a minute as the storm was raging. As the fat raindrops began bombarding the lake, we were surrounded by twelve-inch high splashes of water being kicked up. In the brief shaft of sunlight, from my lake-level viewpoint, these millions of tiny splashes looked like Fourth of July sparklers, going off all around me at once! I've never seen anything like it, before or since. It was breathtaking and I was again humbled by the beauties of nature, you might say. I was happy I was there at that time to experience it.

The storm passed quickly and we got back to fishing. Since the sun was sinking low, getting on toward sunset now, and I was already idling in a large weedy patch, I switched to a yellow and green, froggy-looking cork popper. I'd try some surface fishing and see what happened. On my first cast, I did the textbook thing: I let the popper sit still for the count of ten. Then I gave it a twitch. The water exploded and I was hooked into a big bass. He dove and headed toward deeper water.

I played him for about five minutes without ever seeing him. Was this going to be the eighteen-incher that was our free ticket? I finally reeled him in close enough to get a look; he sure enough looked that big, and more! As I reached to lip him, he flipped and tossed the hook. He finned off into deeper water, looking back over his shoulder like he wanted to kill that big fat, round thing and the guy inside who had disturbed his evening feeding.

#

The Fly Rod Chronicles

As I fell asleep that night, I pondered again the question of pay-as-you-go fishing. It seemed to me the experience on the private lake that day was akin to the blue collar, night crawler chunkin' and dunkin' kind of guy who buys a license (for about the same cost as my rod fee on that little bass lake), fishes on opening day, possibly on July 4 and Labor Day, then hangs it up. Maybe he catches something; maybe he doesn't. It's still a pay-as-you-go fishing world, isn't it?

Unless, of course, you sneak onto someone's privately stocked bass or trout pond. Which, by now, you should certainly know, I don't endorse.

Ask (or pay) first!

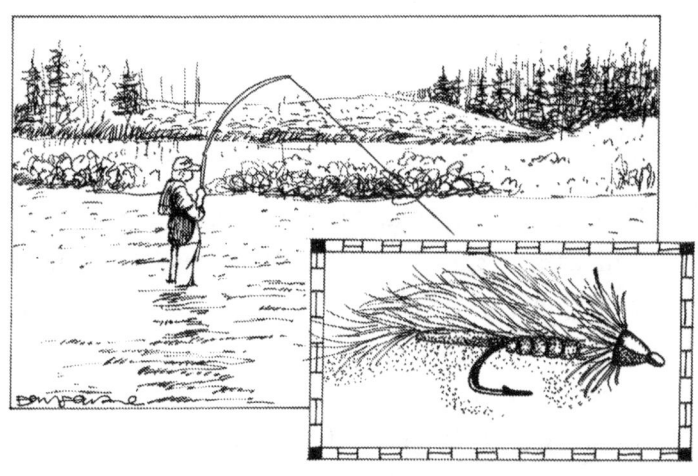

CHAPTER 19

International Diplomacy — A Modest Proposal

(With apologies to Jonathon Swift)

I have a modest proposal to make on the subject of international diplomacy. It seems to me there's a lot of posturing going on here. I mean, W is doing a lot of pulpit-thumping about Iran and Korea. Tony goes before Parliament for his weekly Q&A session and smoothly assures the Members all will be well in the end. Meanwhile, Chirac pouts, the Germans harrumph; Putin consolidates power; China's ticked off at Japan; India quietly grabs more and more outsourcing jobs; the Italians keep turning out expensive suits, shoes, scarves, handbags, and new (German-made) Popes. And we still don't know where Bin Laden's hanging out!

Point is, nothing's getting done. Except a lot of pettifoggery and ruffling feathers, and, with that ruffling, ill will continues to spread; environments remain polluted, human rights continue to be violated at will; and fingers get pointed at everyone and everything except *solutions*. There are a lot of problems in this world and they ain't gettin' fixed, folks.

So, here's my modest proposal: We get all the world's Top Guys (and Gals) together for a fly-fishing fest, say, in Jackson Hole, Wyoming, or West Yellowstone, Montana. September, right after Labor Day, when all the tourists have suffered enough Yellowstone Park gridlock ("But, Mama, we didn't see any *bears*!") and have gone back to Sandgrit, Ohio, or wherever. Shoot, we'll even invite Dick Cheney, since Wyoming's his home state. He can play host (but no shotgun).

Yellowstone and its environs have been returned to the birds and animals, the fish are frantically feeding to fatten for the onslaught of winter, the mornings are frosty, and the trees are turning brilliant. The dust, heat and dullness of summer have given way to fall colors and a last gusher of energy before winter kills everything.

We dress these World Leaders in fly-fishing clothes (from Cabela's, not from the fancy catalogs) and put them all up in

International Diplomacy — A Modest Proposal

the kind of digs where you and I could afford to stay: Best Western, Motel Six, Holiday Inn Express, The Last Roundup Motel and Grille, etc. They have to drive rented cars: a Chevy Malibu, Ford Focus, and so on; no fancy limousines and no chauffeurs.

No Internet access and only local phone calls allowed; check your telephone calling cards and Blackberries at the door. And no staff invited! These folks need to get into the sweet mood that a weekend spent in the Park or thereabouts that time of year brings on.

The food? As much as I love French cuisine, no fancy gourmet cuisine for this trip, no sir! We'll have them dine on a cowboy breakfast to start the day off right: pancakes, bacon, three eggs any style; toast, jam, coffee. For lunch: hamburgers, baked beans, potato chips. Period.

Snacks? You get those at the 7-11 or one of the dozens of other gas and convenience stores in the area, take your pick.

Dinner will be either roast beef, ham, or turkey with dressing, mashed potatoes and gravy; or country-fried steak with sausage gravy over biscuits and canned corn, topped off with pie à la mode (that's the closest they're gonna get to Continental cuisine). A mid-afternoon nap is mandatory, preferably with milk and graham crackers first. Remember how therapeutic that was in kindergarten?

I will humbly volunteer to be their guide; no pay needed, this one's on me. Heck, I'll even loan them the bamboo rods, reels, lines, leaders, flies, etc., from my fishing closet. I've got plenty, or I'll borrow some from Mark and his buddies. They'd be happy to kick in for the sake of furthering international diplomacy, fly-fishing style.

The only shop talk allowed will be limited to asking questions or discussing: wife/husband, kids, and grandkids; soccer scores; the weather; best places to eat or to fish; and favorite rock groups (or other tastes in music), CDs, movies, and the like. No politics or religion allowed!

The first day there will be a very short fly-casting demonstration, also a short demonstration on field emergency hook removal technique. Then everyone will draw real western-grown wheat straws to see who gets matched up with whom for the first day's fishing. There will be no keeping score, you know: most fish caught, biggest fish, and all that silly nonsense that gets in the way of genuine human understanding. They will be allowed to laugh heartily and point fingers if their partner or someone else in the party falls in the river. Drowning partner will be allowed only one internationally recognized obscene finger gesture at the crowd (with appropriate decorum and diplomatic restraint) per dunking. Drenched person must then heartily join in laughter when videos are replayed later that night. Non-dunked partner must make a minimal effort to try to save drenched partner, no matter how much he might secretly be harboring ancient nationalistic, religious or cultural feelings of jealousy, hatred or racism.

All fish caught, if any, will be quickly released in the most compassionate way possible.

At the end of the fete, there'll be a quick spin through the

International Diplomacy — A Modest Proposal

tourist traps to buy tee shirts, Jack-a-lopes, naughty postcards, and such memorabilia for cabinet members, wives (and/or mistresses, if any), staff, kids, or grandkids back home. This will be followed by the mandatory group photo in fishing duds, not suits. No fingers making horns or V signs allowed above neighbors' heads. Well, okay, but use only one hand.

Then, everyone signs the guest comment book and they all promise to do this again next year. The only matter put to a vote is who will be in charge of hosting next year's fishing trip, and where will it be?

Who knows? It may not immediately solve all of the world's major pressing problems, and there are plenty to think about. But it just might bear some fruit by way of promoting international friendship and understanding. At least they'll all have something in common: the language, experience and memories of a few days spent fly fishing together in one of the prettiest places God ever created.

Maybe they'll all go back home, convene their cabinets and parliaments and start out by saying something like: "Guys, let me tell you about the fabulous experience I just had. I went fly fishing. You're not gonna believe the kind of underwear Tony wears! I know; I saw him in the outhouse! But first, let me tell you about the big one I hooked on a fly and almost landed…You should all try it sometime."

Can't ask for much more sweetness than that out of one weekend spent fly fishing.

The Fly Rod Chronicles

CHAPTER 20

Of Dentists' Chairs, Saddles, Waders & Other Things

A s I was sitting in my dentist's chair the other day, waiting for him to start a root canal procedure on a very cranky molar, a deep thought struck me: *Should I go to the bathroom first, or can it wait?* I decided to ask how long I'd be in the saddle. He thought maybe a couple of hours, maybe less; he'd have to see how things looked when he got inside the tooth. I made a quick mental calculation: It takes novocaine about an hour to deaden my mouth, plus another ten to fifteen minutes to "get inside the tooth." Hmmm?

I got up and used the bathroom (just sitting in the chair is enough to bring on the nervous pee-pee's for me).

Standing in the dentist's bathroom, I was struck with the similarity of that moment to being at the car park on your favorite stream. You've driven for an hour, maybe longer. On the way you drank a bevvie, maybe two or three. You're ready to pull on your waders and a similar thought hits you: *Should I go to the bathroom first, or can I wait?*

What about getting stuck on the 405 just south of Long Beach at 5:34 p.m.? Feeling a little stress? Did it occur to you to stop off at the washroom before you left the building and pulled out of the parking lot?

Ever been in a long wedding or funeral service line, the nagging feeling begins, and you squirm uncomfortably wishing the service would end so you could find the restroom?

Did the same thought go through your mind when you sat down for your college entrance exams or finals? Hmmm?

Duh!

There's a principle at work here.

The Canadian Cavalry has a saying: "Never pass up an opportunity to have a pee; you never know how long you'll be in the saddle."

CHAPTER 21

Matthew

It was almost dark as I walked the dirt trail bordering the river, back to my SUV at the car park. I wanted to get on my way while I could safely see the trail. Several weeks before, on a very dark and rainy night on another section of this same river, I learned a hard lesson about caution when I had fallen off an eight-foot levee in the dark and badly hurt one leg. The doctor was surprised I only had a badly sprained knee and ankle and deeply bruised calf muscles.

The Fly Rod Chronicles

"You're (expletive) lucky you didn't come in here with a multiple fracture of your ankle," he'd said.

Late summer, almost fall. Days are shorter; night comes sooner. I'd had a pretty good evening, getting on the Provo just as a multiple hatch was starting—about an hour before dark, just as I had predicted to myself on the drive up. Three kinds of caddis flies, three kinds of mayflies, including some pretty good-sized BWOs; plus two sizes/colors of PMDs were coming off the water. Everywhere you looked there were trout: rolling, sucking down flies, jumping for them. The water was covered with rings of rising trout. It was just one of those sweet, perfect hatches.

I opted to tie on a size 16 post-hackle PMD with a nine-foot leader and 5x tippet. I was using my seven-foot Dickerson (the one Leo dubbed "Stream Master") with a three- weight double taper line. With very little wind, it was working well. In an hour I caught and released several nice browns—I lost count—all of which were over a foot long. I hooked and lost a couple of big boys in the seventeen-inch range. So far it had been a nice evening—great therapy for the soul. And my leg was getting better, almost no pain, although I had hiked over a mile in to a good spot, far beyond all the other fishermen on the river that evening.

As I walked back, enjoying the evening air when there's a zone between cool and warm, I thought about stopping for a couple of casts at that long, flat run just before the car park. I made a deal with myself; it was safe enough to wade in the failing light, so, I'd make just a few casts, but only if nobody

Matthew

else was there first.

As I came around the last bend, past someone's beehives tucked under the ancient overhanging box elder trees, I held my breath. I could hear voices up ahead. I hoped they were walking and not fishing.

There was a teenage boy on the bank, not wearing fly-fishing type clothes, more like he shopped in a Gen-X store. He was talking with another teen wet wading out in the river fishing; he dressed about the same as the first boy. And he was in my spot!

I've fallen lately into the habit of talking to other people I meet on the river. I get a lot of useful information by asking what they're using, what size flies, whether anything is hatching, etc. And sometimes, after a couple hours of solitude, it's just good to be in friendly company again as night starts falling.

I engaged the kid on the bank in conversation. "You guys doing any good?"

"Matt here caught one." The boy on the bank gestured toward his friend in the water.

"Matt!" I called. "How you doin'?"

"Not so good. I can't get them to bite," he responded out of the deepening gloom.

"What you using?" I asked tactfully as possible.

"A big dark nymph. I don't know what it's called." He held up a big black stonefly tied on a size 2 hook. Not good.

"There's a hatch going on. They're hitting dry flies, now, Matt. Little flies, on top of the water."

"Oh. Uh…I don't have any."

"Come on up here. Let me show you what they're hitting."

He waded-splashed over to the bank. I showed him my post wing para-PMD and offered it to him. It was fast getting dark, but Matt had young eyes and steady hands. The fly was soon fixed on his leader; he borrowed and applied some of my Gink.

"All right, Matt. Here would be my strategy if I were you."

He listened intently, head cocked but fidgeting, eager to get out there and catch a fish on that fly.

"You'll want to wade downstream close to the bank about ten yards. Then slowly wade back upstream, angling out a ways, until you're about five yards below any fish you see rising. Got that?"

He nodded. "That close?"

"Sure. It's dark and they're not so shy now. You can get really close. Then cast your fly as close to a spot about two feet above where you last see a fish rise. You'll be casting to a specific target, not just searching all over the place. Try to let the fly down onto the water as softly as possible so you don't spook the fish. If I were you, I'd try up under those overhanging willows. There's always a big boy in there lying up close to the bank. Try a side-arm cast if you can. Good luck."

A lot of information, true, but, as instructed, Matt waded out carefully, got in position and started casting. He was too

Matthew

far below the fish. I urged him to slowly wade a few more steps closer. He did. Then he cast again. Too short. Then the second cast: Right on!

The trout rose and swallowed his fly.

"Got him!" Matt shouted.

As he battled (remembering my prior experience with the Expert), I quietly coached Matt with well-intentioned advice, like: Keep your rod tip up (he was); get him on your reel (blank look); keep him on this side of the river, don't let him get in the swift water over there (he didn't); here's a net if you need one (he did).

Five minutes later, a grinning Matt lifted his seventeen-inch brown out of the net. I loaned him my forceps to remove the fly. He kissed the trout while his buddy took his picture! Then Matt bent to the water with his catch. I coached him to gently rock the fish until it voluntarily left his cradling hands.

He did for a minute. Then, with a flick, the trout moved away from us and sank back into the inky water.

Matt bit the fly off his leader, offering it back to me. I shook my head and handed him a second fly, same pattern.

"For more luck," I said.

The Fly Rod Chronicles

Chapter 22

When I Go

One of the things I like most about fly fishing is the solitude. I love what that word represents. One of my favorite classic Swing-era tunes is Duke Ellington's *Solitude*. The slow, lazy melody, the lyrics, what they mean—so sweet.

When I go on my fly-fishing jaunts, whether it's to a faraway place, or twenty minutes away to fish Big Cottonwood

The Fly Rod Chronicles

Creek, I want to immerse myself in solitude, even if I'm with someone else. You can be alone on the stream, even if you are fishing with someone else.

I can let down the defenses, drop the pretenses, and just be...well, ME.

I can, for example, listen to my heart's content, to my corny jazz and Swing tunes. I can listen to my collection of Ray Conniff CDs without suffering any ribbings from SWAMBO.

I played trombone when I was a kid; still do, sometimes. It was my meal ticket during my high school and community college days. After we got married, I just gave it up; sold my horn to a fat, thirteen-year-old kid to help pay my tuition my last term in law school. Ray Conniff was one of my trombone-playing heroes. Ray and the incomparable J.J. Johnson.

Ray Conniff died recently. Here's a guy who recorded, oh, I don't know, dozens, maybe over a hundred albums; he was still touring, arranging and writing music, playing his horn, strutting his stuff live onstage at age 82. What a guy! He bridged several generations: He came from the Big Band days of the '30s, '40s, and '50s; he played and arranged tunes for the great Artie Shaw ("Begin the Beguine," "Frenesi," "I Cover the Waterfront"), as well as for Johnnie Mathis ("Chances Are"). Yet, Ray's music appealed to millions of young adults and older folks, worldwide. He had a huge audience in Japan, England, Europe, and South America, especially Brazil, where he is still greatly loved.

But this isn't about Ray Conniff, really. Just about *how* I

When I Go

want to go and when.

I have this sort of standing joke with my wife, Janet, about how and when I want to go. I imagine myself at about ninety years old; I can't sleep, I can't pee, I can't eat anything without it upsetting my stomach or something else. I'm pretty crippled with arthritis. I can walk, but it's more like a shuffle. My hearing's bad, my eyesight even worse. But I still love to fly fish even though I can't see to tie on a fly and it hurts my joints and arm muscles a lot to cast a fly rod.

I book a trip to Alberta, a guided float trip on the Bow River. It's going to be my last fishing trip.

I hook into one giant brown, the kind of which legends are made. After my last fight with that trout, maybe an enjoyable ten minutes (since this is my last fight, I stretch it out as long as possible). I sort of lean out over the gunwales and let him pull me overboard. They find my body a couple of days later about a mile downstream. I'm still tightly clutching my fly rod, with a smile on my face. Attached to the end of the line is this giant brown, dead now, but with this very confused expression on its face.

In other words, I want to go out raging "against the dying of the light."

I want to know that I gave Life all it could handle.

That I never quit, never gave up enjoying every day, every moment, every contact with family, friends, business partners, neighbors, fishing guides, even strangers like Matthew.

That I never stopped being curious; that I never ceased to be surprised by the intricate physics and the simple beauty, the colors of a rainbow right after a summer thunder shower.

That I never hardened my heart.

That I always felt gooey inside whenever I heard a Bach cello partita.

That I never stopped being awed by the colorings, the pretty markings of rainbow, brook, and brown trout.

That even though I preferred blue jeans and sweatshirts, I secretly took a little pride in being able to tie a perfect dimpled knot in my necktie.

That I took great comfort in rubbing my hand over the silky finish of a fine bamboo fly rod. The same for my many pet dogs through the years.

That I never stopped being grateful for any small act of kindness shown to me, for any gift however small.

That I always felt humbled, yet inspired, when looking at a Monet painting. And I can say the same for Utah's Canyonlands.

That I had a strong sense of family: a real feeling of connection with my staunch and brave ancestors from many lands and cultures who mingled their blood so that I became who I am.

That I never ceased to be amazed at how lucky I was to be a father. That I considered myself lucky for my marvelous, beautiful, intelligent, talented children and grandchildren. That I was humbled by being able to witness many of their miraculous births.

That I always felt humbled by my small place in this great universe.

When I Go

That from the first time I saw Janet, until my last breath, I was totally turned on by her.

WHEN I GO

A poem by Richard Landerman

I love wood. So when I go
Nestle me in simple pine
To keep me warm.
I will touch its honey planks
And find much comfort there.

I love music. So when I go
Bring some bagpipes. Or, better yet:
Two trombones, drums and a cornet.
A reedy clarinet to lead the way,
Wailing out St. James's Infirmary.

I love flowers. So when I go

The Fly Rod Chronicles

*Plant me a few, sweet violets
And daffodils for spring. Spicy dianthus
For June. And pungent chrysanthemums,
Yes, mums, orange and red and gold for fall.*

*I love children. So when I go
Let them play upon my grave.
Let them dance upon my grave
While you tell them I was brave
And generous and true.*

*That when I went
I spoke of you.
That when I went
I spoke only of you.*

www.ingramcontent.com/pod-product-compliance
Lightning Source LLC
Chambersburg PA
CBHW051429290426
44109CB00016B/1485